JARGON 100

Sponsors to the Edition
Donald B. Anderson and
Sally Midgette Anderson

National Patrons of THE JARGON SOCIETY
1984–1985

From This "Condensery: / The Complete Writing of Lorine Niedecker

edited by
Robert J. Bertholf

1985   The Jargon Society

Dedication

for
Susan Howe
my guide through these poems

Contents

xi

FOR PAUL AND OTHER POEMS 35

THE YEARS GO BY   75

IN EXCHANGE FOR HAIKU 117

HOME / WORLD 127

NORTH CENTRAL   159

OTHER WRITING 229

NOTES   311

Introduction

Lorine Niedecker is a poet of a single loca-
tion, the area around Blackhawk Island, not
far from Fort Atkinson, Wisconsin. She spent
most of her life on the island, near where the
Rock River empties into Lake Koshkonong.
The subject matter of the flooding river, the
human labor in each season, birds and ani-
mals, the flowers and trees of the area inform
her poetry at every point. She achieves a
form that convinces in its presentation, but
never relinquishes her firm and intelligent
grasp of the actual. Life along the river, she
writes "gave me life/ give me this/ our rela-
tive the air/floods/our rich friend/silt."
She attended primary and secondary school at
Fort Atkinson, and then Beloit College for
two years, 1922–1924. She returned home
when her mother's failing hearing made her
presence necessary. The biographical infor-
mation is sketchy. She was a studious and sol-
itary person, talented at the piano and in
choral singing, but not gregarious. She chose
life by the river. There was a short, failed
marriage in 1928, and also work as a library
assistant in the Dwight Foster Public Library
in Fort Atkinson 1928–1930. She began to
appear in the literary magazines in the 1930s,
and began writing radio plays in the same
decade, which led to employment at Station
WHA in Madison from 1942–1944. From
1944 to 1950 she worked for Hoard's Dairy-
man, where she became a proofreader. "I
worked in the print shop," she writes,

> right down among em
> the folk from whom all poetry flows
> and dreadfully much else.
>   . . .

What would they say if they knew
I sit for two months on six lines
of poetry?

Early in her career she began writing to
Louis Zukofsky, and claimed that without the
Objectivist issue of *Poetry* (February, 1931)
she would not have become a writer. The
early letters to Zukofsky are those of a
daughter writing to a father, a fledgling poet
to a mentor. Zukofsky's influence was im-
mense, mainly in the instructions to tighten
and condense her line, in concentrating on
the most specific means of expression. By
1946 she had enough poems for a volume,
New Goose, published by James A. Decker.
The next book would not appear until 1961,
when the Wild Hawthorn Press of Edin-
burgh, Scotland brought out the small vol-
ume, *My Friend Tree*. Edward Dorn wrote an
introduction to that volume, mainly, he said
much later, because he was attracted to Nie-
decker's use of the sentence as the unit of
composition and not necessarily the single
line.

In 1951 her mother, Daisy Niedecker, died,
totally deaf, and her father, fatigued by a life
of work and shocked by his wife's death, died
in 1954. Lorine inherited two houses on
Blackhawk Island. The obligations of owner-
ship, renting, seeing to the plumbing, and
foreclosing come into the poems. From 1957
to 1962 she was employed by the Fort Atkin-
son Memorial Hospital, as a cleaning person.
She remained in that job until she married
Albert Millen in May, 1963. They lived for a
time in Milwaukee, but when Albert retired
they built a house by the river and returned
to the place of her special habitation. Albert
was a companion, and showed her new sights
on trips to South Dakota and around Lake
Superior.

In the 1950s she took up a correspondence
with Cid Corman, and many of her poems

appeared in the magazine, *Origin*. During this period, and into the 1960s, she wrote sequences of poems, many of them centering on Paul Zukofsky, the violinist son of Louis Zukofsky. But it was not until the late 1960s that larger selections of her poems found a wider audience. *North Central* was published by Fulcrum Press in 1968, *T&G* by the Jargon Society in 1969, and, finally, *My Life By Water: Collected Poems 1936–1968* by the Fulcrum Press in 1970. Three completed manuscripts were left after her death on 31 December 1970: "Earth and Its Atmosphere" and "Harpsichord & Salt Fish," and "The Very Veery."

That she chose a solitary life in a single locality does not indicate a set of cloistered interests. She knew the specific geological and environmental factors of her landscape and honored their strength:

> *In every part of every living thing*
> *is stuff that once was rock*
>
> *In blood the minerals*
> *of rock*

She also knew her region's history, as she writes of Thure Kumlien in "I'd like to tell you about a man," and Ansom Dart in "Pioneers." She uncovered the history and forces of nature in land and water and made them forces in her poetry. "My life is hung up/in the flood/a wave blurred." But she was also a reader. Her letters tell of book-buying trips to Madison and to Fort Atkinson; they also tell of reading Plotinus, Swedenborg, Freud's letters, D.H. Lawrence's letters, the Adams-Jefferson correspondence, Edith Sitwell's *Taken Care Of*, and T.S. Eliot's *Murder in the Cathedral*. In a letter to Cid Corman dated 18 February 1962, she gives a profile of her library:

> You now inhabit a corner of my immortal cupboard with LZ (especially the

short poems), Emily Dickinson, Thoreau, Lucretius, Marcus Aurelius, John Muir, bits of Santayana, D.H. Lawrence, Dahlberg, William Carlos Williams, and haiku.

She had read Wordsworth, as well as Audubon, Linnaeus, and other naturalists. Her familiarity with the works of Darwin and the letters of William Morris is evident in the lines and titles of two late poems.

After the major influence of Zukofsky, William Carlos Williams' was next in importance to Niedecker's poetic life. The formalities of his poems centered her attention. Williams' three-part line enters her work too, but modified into a unit of composition, a sentence-length stanza, only slightly punctuated. As she wrote in a letter to Zukofsky dated November 1949, "I see what you say, 'don't bother with punctuation if the form is inevitable'—I guess you've got something there." She began to develop indigenous rhythmic structures from her line breaks, which, through patterns of repetition, specified a stable form. Stanza added to stanza, adding up to sequences, prepared the way for grand formal achievements in the longer poems "Wintergreen Ridge" and "Paean to Place." Her poetry follows a course of outward expansion. The line of her very early poems directed itself inward as a part of the stanza. But the stanzas themselves, as she matured, began reaching beyond their own immediacy to the external world. It should come as no surprise then that in her later poems, she became preoccupied with the processes of perception and the natural generation of form.

She was never *isolate*. Well informed about national and international events, she knew something of music (and admired it), listened intelligently to radio and TV. Like Emily Dickinson, her only likely antecedent, she

chose her way of life in order to fulfill her po-
etry. She learned the poet's work, "to sit at
desk/and condense," and "from this conden-
sery" has come a magnificent expansion of
the imagination's life.

This book brings together the collected and
the uncollected writing of Lorine Niedecker.
That she wrote plays, narratives and critical
prose is not well known. She chose writing
first, above the possible fortune of guaranteed
employment and the possible fame of a public
life of letters. A statement to Jonathan Wil-
liams, in a letter dated 10 January 1957, is
very specific: "Poetry is the most important
thing in my life." Her commitment to poetry
was complete, and her dedication to the art of
writing intense.

My aim here is not only to collect, but to
present all the writing of Lorine Niedecker in
a manner faithful to the last intentions of
their author. This is not easy. Niedecker re-
wrote, condensed, and re-arranged her work
so often that even the last typed copy of a
poem does not represent its final state, only a
version conceived of at that given moment.
My Life By Water: Collected Poems 1936–1968
(London: Fulcrum Press, 1970) was the larg-
est collection of writing that Niedecker
proofread. She was pleased with its presenta-
tion, and therefore I have accepted it as the
basic text and configuration of poems for this
edition.

The textual orders are problematic; they
will always remain so. Poems published in
earlier books found themselves re-configured
in new collections, given sequences were re-
arranged when they passed from magazine
publication to book publication, and even
from book to book. For this reason the last
appearance of a text is assumed to be the pre-
ferred. And when this has involved exclu-
sions, I have appended them to the most
recent state of their original sequences. Where
there were more recent typescripts, as was

the case with "Earth and Its Atmosphere" and "Harpsichord & Salt Fish," I have taken the texts and configurations of the typescript to be the author's intended version, even when they displace versions in print. For those poems Lorine Niedecker left out of *My Life By Water* and those that appear only in manuscript, I have attempted a chronological order. What is obvious, however, is that she herself was continually involved in creating sequential formalities and contexts. She was more concerned with her order than with an exact chronological order.

The most notable example of this is "For Paul." Miss Niedecker sent many of these poems in manuscript to Louis Zukofsky, who dated them as he received them. So it is possible to determine an accurate chronology. Initially there were eight numbered Groups. Unfortunately, Group V has not been found, which leaves seven distinct sequences, each arranged by their poet. Groups I and II were published as Groups. There are manuscript versions of all the surviving sequences, and except for Groups I and II, these have supplied the texts presented here. Sometimes the same poems appear in a different arrangement in different sequences, indicating a slightly different thematic and contextual locus of meaning and form.

Chronological order, it goes without saying, is often at odds with the order of book, magazine, or even manuscript appearances. Another case in point is "In Exchange for Haiku." A manuscript exists in which far more poems are included in this sequence than ever appeared in print. Different edited versions of the larger, unpublished compilation came out in *Origin*, and in *My Life By Water*. Another reworking entitled "Poems from the Porthole" was included in the typescript, "Harpsichord & Salt Fish," and it restores sections omitted from the original, much older sequence. Not only were poems arranged and rearranged over the years, but so were occasional stanzas, often cut free and removed to a different context in their original sequence, or to a completely new one.

I have tried to maintain the integrity of all sequences found in the manuscripts, and when I was able to determine that the poet meant a poem to be autonomous as well as a part of some sequence, I have also represented it in a later section of this edition. Then too Niedecker also removed poems from their original contexts and published them in magazines and books on their own. This practice makes the appearance of individual poems in separate sections even more necessary. And without which, her feelings for sequential form is completely lost.

This duplication of single poems within and without sequences honors both editorial principles of this edition: to present as full a record of Niedecker's writing as possible; and to present her last intention for each poem's configuration and form.

In some instances, like the four poems, "Dear Paul," I have included the earliest manuscript version, published version, a second published version, and then the later manuscript version. In the process of this poem, as in the processes of others like "What's wrong with marriage," "Yes, my time's waste" and "The Eye," Niedecker's habits of revision are very apparent. These multiple versions clearly demonstrate her process of condensing, and the eventual condensation, that practice most central to her art.

Notes have been provided to give information about variants of individual poems. When the pieces are uncollected, notes specify first appearances. Some annotations have been included when they clarify a poem's

context, but I have resisted the temptation to
make textual glosses. That is a task for a dif-
ferent kind of book.

R. J. B.
The Poetry/Rare Books Collection
The University at Buffalo
State University of New York

Acknowledgements

This edition of the writing of Lorine Niedecker could not have been finished without the assistance of many people. I especially thank John Chalmers and Cathy Henderson of the Harry Ransom Humanities Research Center, The University of Texas at Austin, Howard B. Gotlieb, of the Special Collection Mugar Memorial Library, Boston University, and Lola L. Szladits, Curator of The Berg Collection, New York Public Library. Cid Corman, the Literary Executor of Lorine Niedecker's estate, assisted in many ways, as did Jonathan Williams. I am indebted to Lisa Faranda for very helpful advice, and to Jane Knox for very specific biographical information. Stephen Jama supplied a copy of a poem from his private collection, James Weil of The Elizabeth Press and Jim Lowell of The Asphodel Book Shop offered sustaining encouragements. I am most grateful to Diane Morris, Eileen Basinski, and the staff of The Poetry/Rare Books Collection, The University at Buffalo, State University of New York for assistance in preparing the manuscript.

From This
Condensery:
The Complete
Writing of
Lorine Niedecker

Early Poems

Wasted Energy

Refinement of speech is a thing that we preach
All in vain it would sometimes seem,
For this is the age when slang is the rage,
And vocabularies, a dream.

I used to make rhymes; now I hand people lines
(And they're boresome and foolish, no doubt),
But however folks feel—one thing is so real—
A great many "expire and pass out."

When Tom, Dick and Phil are conversing,
The effect is entirely unique,
We can't quite make out what they're talking about
But we gather it's Sheba or Sheik.

I tell Tom of the quake that made Mexico shake.
"Well, ain't that the berries?" quotes he.
When describing a quail or a sunset or whale—
They're "wonderful!"—each of the three.

It's amazingly queer, but from all sides we hear
Of the "crooks" and "tough birds" in our town,
Of "wild women," of "guys," many "I wonder why's,"
"Juicy" tales and requests to "pipe down."

Any brains do you say? You may put them away
By this modernized method of talk.
An argument clinch? Say, "Oh, yes, that's a cinch,"
"Absolutely" is still better—less thought.

The American tongue is found lacking by some,
So they take a few words from afar.
But "Pas auf" and "trez bean" are as common, 'twould seem,
As Uncle Joe Cannon's cigar.

o

Mourning Dove

The sound of a mourning dove
slows the dawn
there is a dee round silence
in the sound.

Or it may be I face the dull prospect
of an imagist
turned philosopher

o

Transition

Colors of October
wait with easy dignity
for the big game—
like gorgeous quill-pens
in old inkwells
almost dry.

o

SPIRALS

Promise of Brilliant Funeral

Travel, said he of the broken umbrella, enervates
the point of stop; once indoors, theology,
for want of a longer telescope, is made
of the moon-woman passing amid silk
nerve-thoughts in the blood.
(There's trouble with the moon-maker's union,
the blood-maker's union, the thought-maker's union;
but the play could be altered.)

A man strolls pale among zinnias,
life and satin sleeves renounced.
He is intent no longer on what direction herons fly
in hell, but on computing space in forty minutes,
and ascertains at the end of the path:
this going without tea holds a hope of tasting it.
(Chalk-faces going down in rows before a stage
have seen no action yet.)

o

Mr. Brown visits home.
His broker by telephone advises him it's night
and a plum falls on a marshmallow
and sight comes to owls.
He risks three rooms noisily for the brightest sconce.
Rome was never like this.

(The playwright dies in the draft
when ghosts laugh.)

o

When Ecstasy is Inconvenient

Feign a great calm;
all gay transport soon ends.
Chant: who knows—
flight's end or flight's beginning
for the resting gull?

Heart, be still.
Say there is money but it rusted;
say the time of moon is not right for escape.
It's the color in the lower sky
too broadly suffused,
or the wind in my tie.

Know amazedly how
often one takes his madness
into his own hands
and keeps it.

o

MOTHER GEESE

O let's glee glow as we go
there must be things in the world—
Jesus pay for the working soul,
fearful lives by what right hopeful
and the apse in the tiger's horn,
costume for skiing I have heard
and rings for church people
and glee glo glum
it must be fun
to have boots for snow.
o

She had tumult of the brain
and I had rats in the rain
and she and I and the furlined man
were out for gain
o

There's a better shine
on the pendulum
than is on my hair
and many's the time
. . . .
I've seen it there.
o

Scuttle up the workshop,
settle down the dew,
I'll tell you what my name is
when we've made the world new.
o

My coat threadbare
over and down capital hill,
fashions mornings after.

In this Eternal Category's
land of rigmarole
see thru the laughter.
o

The land of four o'clocks is here
the five of us together
        looking for our supper.
Half past endive, quarter to beets,
seven milks, ten cents cheese,
        lost, our land, forever.

o

LADY IN THE LEOPARD COAT

Tender spotted
hoped with care
she's coming back
from going there.

o

FASCIST FESTIVAL

The music, lady,
you demand—
the brass
breaks my hand.

o

To war they kept
            us going
but when the garden
            bloomed
I let them know
            my death.

With time war
            is splendid
and the rainbow
            sword,
they do not break
            my rest,

o

Petrou his name was sorrow
and little did he know
they called him Tomorrow
and Today let him go.

o

The eleventh of progressional
the make-believe of prayer,
too many dunderoos
and everybody there.

If you stay at home
loving in the light
you'll always get an answer
wrong or right.

o

In speaking spokes the mighty
come down from welding wires
to light up the farmers
with electricity.

For sun and moon and radio
farmers pay dearly;
their natural resource: turn
the world off early.

o

Young girl to marry,
winds the washing harry.
o

Missus Dorra
came to town
to buy some silkalene.
The clerk said Oh
my dear Mrs. Morra
is it in style ageen?

All these years
I saved and saved
and saved my silkalene
and yesterday
I threw it away—
how would taffeta be?

No, taffeta
cracks from hanging, besides
it's not being worn.
Mrs. Porra my dear
if you're going to be hung
won't crêpe do as weel?
o

Motor cars
      like china
sometimes chink each other.
Will the sugar bowl
of taffy color
      speeding
stop to eat people?
o

I spent my money
by the ocean
and have not any
to fill a tooth.
o

Trees over the roof
and I was down
when the night
came in.
o

NEWS

To wit, the lever said.

As a young woman
I saw that

done

no child
no enlightenment.

We approach the dignity
of the ad.

Or successfully maintain
a humorous relation

between the ayes
and the nose

(got to give the asses
an eye)

Faces slander
O I see
faces
slander.

Find body
of ashamed man.

Labor leader flogged to death,
believed in destroying home, church
and civilization, radio caster said,
no right thinking people
could deny it
said

People should know
who the floggers are

how the air mind
gets a raise

and the extravagant
broadcast
without mercy.

The issue wouldn't have been brought up
if your husband hadn't been killed.

The police described him
as an intelligent man.

Lilies
of the kind

look   she's right.

The flag   go hang

in the war market
to which the farmers
of this country
bring their products.

Duck
wobbler
for all intentions.

They separated
not legally,
the world has no notice.
His old wife illegally starves

his mother
nothing left
eats
dies.

You
got food?

I'd like to keep my hat and coat
reasonably clean
on the walk from New York
to California gate unless I get work—
will pay $10.

My shoulder worn

over and down Payroll Hill

fashions mornings after.

Raw wind, rain,
one month going into another
what the hell

Frail limbs are proportionately low
Buy a limb today.

And while we walk
we ride

footgear alert
to beat the sweet tenor
of their sentiment
(they keep their trees
away from us)

a tour of the tines
rise and sore

life term.
o

WILL YOU WRITE ME A CHRISTMAS POEM?

Will I!

The mad stimulus of Gay Gaunt Day
meet to put holly on a tree
and trim green bells
and trim green bells

Now candles come to faces.
You are wrong to-day
you are wrong to-day,
my dear. My dear—

One translucent morning
in the damp development of winter,
one fog to move a city backward—
Backward, backwards, backward!

You see the objects and the movable fingers,
Candy dripping from branches,
Horoscopes of summer
and you don't have Christmas ultimately—
Ultima Thule ultimately!

Spreads and whimpets
Good to the cherry drops,
Whom for a splendor
Whom for a splendor

I'm going off the paper I'm going off the pap-

Send two birds out
Send two birds out
And carol them in,
Cookies go round.

What a scandal is Christmas,
What a scandle Christmas is
a red stick-up
to a lily.

You flagellate my woes, you flagellate,
I interpret yours,
holly is a care divine
                holly is a care divine

and where are we all from here.
Drink for there is nothing else to do
but pray,
And where are we?

Throw out the ribbons
and tie your people in
All spans dissever
once the New Year opens
and snow derides
a doorway,
it spasms dissever

All spans dissever,
wherefore we, for instance, recuperate
no grief to modulate
no grief to modulate

The Christian cacophony
one word to another,
sound of gilt trailing the world
slippers to presume,
postludes, homiclea, sweet tenses
imbecile and corrupt,—
        failing the whirled, trailing the whirlled

This great eventual heyday
to plenty the hour thereof,
fidelius.
Heyday! Hey-day! Hey-day!

I fade the color of my wine
that an afternoon might live
foiled with shine and brittle
I fade the color of my wine

Harmony in Egypt,
representative birthday.
Christ what a destiny
What a destiny's Christ's, Christ!

۹

Hop press
        and conveyor for a hearse,
Newall Carpenter Senior's
           two patented works.

Kilbourne. Eighteen sixty-eight.
Twelve hundred women and boys hopped.
When the market raced down to a dime a pound
from sixty-five cents, planters who'd staked
all they had, stopped.

o

For sun and moon and radio
farmers pay dearly;
their natural resource: turn
the world off early.

o

A lawnmower's one of the babies I'd have
if they'd give me a job and I didn't get bombed
in the high grass

by the private woods. Getting so
when I look off my space I see waste
I'd like to mow.

o

Du Bay

He kept a grog shop, this fur trader killer?
Defense: Any fur trader would
to make merchandise go. Moses Strong:
Inquire if the liquor was good.

He called Chief Oshkosh's daughter his wife?
Irrelevant! —John B. Du Bay
shot a man for claiming his land, enough
the possession of real estate.

Witnesses judged him as good as the average
for humanity, honesty, peace.
The court sent him home to his children,
his dogs, his gun, and his geese.
o

Here it gives the laws for fishing thru the ice—
only one hook to a line,
stay at the hole, can't go in to warm up,
well, we never go fishing, so they can't catch us.
o

On Columbus Day he set out for the north
to inspect his forty acres,
brought back a plaster of Paris deer-head
and food from the grocers and bakers,

a wall-thermometer to tell if he's cold,
a new kind of paring knife,
and painted in red, a bluebottle gentian
for the queen, his wife.
o

I said to my head, Write something.
It looked me dead in the face.
Look around, dear head, you've never read
of the ground that takes you away.
Speed up, speed up, the frosted windshield's
                    a fern spray.
o

Hand Crocheted Rug

Gather all the old, rip and sew
the skirt I've saved so long,
Sally's valance, the twins' first calico
and the rest I worked to dye.
Red, green, black, hook,
hitch, nevermind, cramped
around back not yet the turn
of the century . . . Grandpa forward
from the shop, "Ought to have a machine."
o

They came at a pace
to go to war.

They came to more:
a leg brought back
to a face.

o

I doubt I'll get silk stockings out
of my asparagus
that grows too fast to stop it,
or any pair of Capital's
miracles of profit.

o

A monster owl
out on the fence
flew away. What
is it the sign
of? The sign of
an owl.

o

Birds' mating-fight
feathers floating down
offspring started
toward the ground.
o

From my bed I see
the wind willow
the grass.

From my head
in feathers comes
a gas.

I think of a tree
to make it
last.
o

What a woman!—hooks men like rugs,
clips as she hooks, prefers old wool, but all
childlike, lost, houseowning or pensioned men
her prey. She covets the gold in her husband's teeth.
She'd sell dirt, she'd sell your eyes fried in deep grief.
o

The brown muskrat, noiseless,
swims the white stream,
stretched out as if already
a woman's neck-piece.

In Red Russia the Russians
at a mile a minute
pitch back Nazi wildmen
wearing women.
o

My friend tree
I sawed you down
but I must attend
an older friend
the sun
o

Along the river
        wild sunflowers
over my head
        the dead
who gave me life
        give me this
our relative the air
        floods
our rich friend
        silt
o

The broad-leaved Arrow-head
grows vivid and strong
in my book, says: underneath
the surface of the stream the leaves
are narrow, long.
I don't investigate,
mark the page . . . I suppose
if I sat down beside a frost
and had no printed sign
I'd be lost. Well, up
from lying double in a book,
go long like a tree
and broad as the library.

o

Black Hawk held: In reason
land cannot be sold,
only things to be carried away,
and I am old.

Young Lincoln's general moved,
pawpaw in bloom,
and to this day, Black Hawk,
reason has small room.

o

Remember my little granite pail?
The handle of it was blue.
Think what's got away in my life—
Was enough to carry me thru.

o

Ash woods, willows close to shore,
gentle overflow each spring,
here he lived to be eighty-four
then left everything.

Heirs rush in—lay one tree bare
claiming a birdhouse, leave
wornout roof hanging there,
nothing underneath.

If he could come back and see his place
fought over that he'd held apart
he'd say: all my life I saved,
now twitter, my heart.

He owned these woods, every board,
till he lost his spring and fall.
If he could say: trees craved for—
overflow to all.

o

Audubon

Tried selling my pictures. In jail
twice for debt. My companion
a sharp, frosty gale.

       In England unpacked
with fear:
must I migrate back

to the woods unknown, strange
to all but the birds
I paint?

Dear Lucy, the servants here
move quiet
as killdeer.

o

Gen. Rodimstev's story
  (Stalingrad)

Four of us lived off half an acre
till grandfather traded it
for a gallon of liquor.

White Guards flogged father to death,
I studied to save
man's sweet breath.

o

Bombings

You could go to the Underground's platform
for a three half-penny tube fare;
safe vaults of the Bank of England
you couldn't go there.

The sheltered slept
under eiderdown,
Lady Diana and the Lord himself
in apartments deep in the ground.

o

To see the man who took care of our stock
as we slept in the dark, the backbirds flying
high as the market out of our pie,
I travel now at crash of day
on the el, a low rush of geese over those below,
to see the man who smiled
and gave us a first-hand country shake.

o

The museum man!
I wish he'd take Pa's spitbox!
I'm going to take that spitbox out
and bury it in the ground
and put a stone on top.
Because without that stone on top
it would come back.

o

Mr. Van Ess bought 14 washcloths?
Fourteen washrags, Ed Van Ess?
Must be going to give em
to the church, I guess.

He drinks, you know. The day we moved
he came into the kitchen stewed,
mixed things up for my sister Grace—
put the spices in the wrong place.

o

Don't shoot the rail!
Let your grandfather rest!
Tho he sees your wild eyes
he's falling asleep,
his long-billed pipe
on his red–brown vest.

o

Asa Gray wrote Increase Lapham:
pay particular attention
to my pets, the grasses.

o

Not feeling well, my wood uncut.
                              And why?
The street's bare-legged young girls
       in my eye
with their bottoms out (at home they wear
                              long robes).
              My galoshes
          chopped the cold
till cards in The Moon where I sawed my mouth
                    to make the bid.
And now my stove's too empty
       to be wife and kid.
       o

I wrote another,
longer, starting

Homage
of love for, to
the young

but the pain's too much now,
for me to copy.
       o

Grampa's got his old age pension,
$15 a month,
his own food and place.

But here he comes,
fiddle and spitbox . . .

Tho't I'd stop with you a little,
Harriut,
you kin have all I got.
o

My man says the wind blows from the south,
      we go out fishing, he has no luck,
        I catch a dozen, that burns him up,
I face the east and the wind's in my mouth,
but my man has to have it in the south.
o

I'm a sharecropper
down here in the south.
Housing conditions arc grave.

We've a few long houses
but most folks, like me,
make a home out of barrel and stave.
o

A working man appeared in the street
in soldiers suit, no work, no peace.
What'r you doing in that dress,
a policeman said, where's the fight?
And after they took him for a ride
in the ambulance, they made arrest
for failure to molest.
    o

We know him—Law and Order League—
fishing from our dock,
testified against the pickets
at the plant—owns stock.

There he sits and fishes
stiff as if a stork
brought him, never sprang from work—
a sport.
    o

That woman! —eyeing houses.
She's moved in on my own poor guy.
    She held his hand and told him where to sign.

He gives up costs on his tree-covered shack—
insurance against wind, fire, falling aircraft, riots—
    home itself, was our break in the thick.

Because look! How can she keep it?—
to hold a house has to rent it out
        and spend her life on the street.
o

Van Gogh

At times I sit in the dunes,
faint, not enough to eat.
The path thru the dunes
is like a desert   the family's shoes
patched and worn and many more
such views.
o

The clothesline post is set
yet no totem-carvings distinguish the Niedecker tribe
from the rest; every seventh day they wash:
worship sun; fear rain, their neighbors' eyes;
raise their hands from ground to sky,
and hang or fall by the whiteness of their all.
o

He built four houses
to keep his life.
Three got away
before he was old.

He wonders now
rocking his chair
should he have built
a boat

dipping, dipping
and sitting so.
o

Well, spring overflows the land,
floods floor, pump, wash machine
of the woman moored to this low shore by deafness.

    Good-bye to lilacs by the door
    and all I planted for the eye.
    If I could hear—too much talk in the world,
    too much wind washing, washing
    good black dirt away.

Her hair is high.
Big blind ears.

    I've wasted my whole life in water.
    My man's got nothing but leaky boats.
    My daughter, writer, sits and floats.
o

Pioneers

Anson Dart pierced the forest,
                    fell upon wild strawberries.
Frosts, fires, land speculation, comet.
                         Corn to be planted.
How to keep the strawberries?—
                    Indians' sugar full of dirt.
How to keep the earth.

Winnebagoes knew nothing
of government purchase of their land,
agency men got chiefs drunk
then let them stand.

On the steamer *Consolation*
            came Dart's wife and daughters,
already there his sons and three sides of the house.
In the Great Bitter Winter a rug closed the side
                         that was bare.
For mortar they bored out a white-oak log,
pounded enough corn for a breakfast Johnnie cake
by rising—all sons—at 4:00.
Could be more, could be warmer, could be more.
Sun, turn the earth once more.

Between fighting fourteen nations' invading troops
and starting the first thousand-acre farms
      we hungered,
an effort to rise or stand up straight.

A tractor has seven hundred fifteen parts.
            I studied—
I'm a Morvin from the Eraya tribe—
                  learned all about oil and sand
the whole inner essence of the core.
Gorky recalls Professor Hvolson
                    lecturing on Einstein,
clung with his hands to the pulpit,
swayed back and forth from lack of food.
Then—the first one! —red wheels
            dipped, met the earth.
Red wheels gave the earth a new turn.
o

(L.Z.)

"An acre of music"
or a room closer to it
movement, rest, repeat,
for those making music
but not allowed to hear it
and those in peril
on the street

o

New!
Reason explodes. Atomic split
shows one element
Jew

Now hide
who can bombarded particles
of international
pride

o

Old man who seined
to educate his daughter
sees red Mars rise:
            What lies
behind it?

Cold water business
now starred in Fishes
of dipnet shape
                to ache
thru his arms.
o

You are my friend—
you bring me peaches
and the high bush cranberry
                you carry
my fishpole

you water my worms.
you patch my boot
with your mending kit
            nothing in it
but my hand
o

For Paul

1.

Dear Paul:
the sheets of your father's book of poetry
are bound for England?
At last, after the hardships

he can say, "take back to your ship
a gift from me,
something precious, a real good thing . . .
such as a friend gives to a friend."

You ask what kind of boats in *my* country
on my little river.
Black as those beside Troy
but sailless tar-preserve-black fish barges
and orange and Chinese-red rowboats
in which the three virtues
            knowledge, humanity, energy
infrequently ride.

Ask me rather what kind of people
            —here they kick the book of poetry open—
because you can't keep people from water
they'll cut through to it
rut through in the soft
dig under and come up in the middle,
by water they go for Helen
in water seek their own image
fish Sunday's quiet
by water uncork their beer
on days off
                  to see light behave
                  double moon on the wave
water where bobbed likely the first life on earth.
Right of way—
you can't keep em from it.

Ask me what kind of children.
Who are the kids of the calm-moving wet,
of Saturday-Sunday parents.
One with listening eyes like yours
little Sat Sun shall we say
sits in the thinning wild rice
watching wide sky wash
away from the laundry.
One.

What we have is the Sunday school crowd
laying waste the countryside
with their long sticks.
Beat the grass
whip Queen Anne's lace
bow low, my family of young poplars
oh holy day

The sons and the daughters
on their way to water,
your floaters, your doters,
your wigglers, your little pond scum
turtle torturers, danglers of frogs
in any mud puddle
your wuttle-gutt goop longs
            —they can't talk—
the pings and the ack acks
dealing death to the little green thing
cute kids
kee-yute tribe
who at six steer the motor boat
straight to the dock

No they can't talk
they combust
or they mush it

Reggy's the spitwit kid
chewer of seaweed inland
        juices, breaks up into acids
related to what was his name
            who could speak no English
            his tongue runneth all on buttered fish
yet asleep in his army blankets
as sweet a child as any

And there's always the army
to make a man of him.
Take his brother, 19,
no better butter–mutter
no clear song, fished out
left town
        empty in the head
                swish swash
but good with three bullets on a knife

        After me
                backward
                        the cockpit
                                fell out

        Give me silk
                or nylon
                        and down
                                with your art

You saw Guppy the fleet type submarine, Paul
I give you Gulpy

To hear him
he could hold up his arm
and keep the bomb from falling
or he could drop it.

Frog jabber
grab her
she's mine to pierce
ready for love

Gloater, soaker, roaring river boater
emptied, poured out, done,
stick out your tongue
mammoth oar-muscle baby

The day of the giant armored fishes
                was a clear thing

Five-year-old Chief Noise
guns strewn over his lawn
his uncle a Justice
held us up one night by the garden gate
throws the cat by the tail at noon
cries to get her in out of the rain
                after dark

He'll take no backwash from anybody

What does the father do?
                He steals. I mean
                he works for a steel company.
Well, why not? –
Steals from himself
as they from him
his time, his life.
His pleasure in his work
                flows by.

He's left loved
for the spending of his wages
                on things he won't want.

The elegant office girl
is power-rigged.

She carries her nylon hard-pointed
breast uplift
like parachutes
half-pulled.

All children begin with the life of the mind—
if there were no marsh or stream
imagine it

---

99 children go into business
                                selling angleworms,
the hundredth develops free fingers in John Sebastian Brook

Boys who play the fiddle never amount to anything
the storekeeper screamed
with the radio in his face
so he raised his son to shop work
turn screws, grind scissors
and in the end own stores
                force his rivals to the wall then buy em out
                        selling and buying
                        how are you dying
                            worn out at fifty
                                nevermind the mind

while poets and players
of serious song
stand the stress

All along the water
50,000 crusading children
beat their way to the pretty sea shells.
Find yourself a starfish and you'll see the sea open.
And still there's no miracle.
Sold into slavery
sold

Brother
            sold to the factory assembly line
            for 'a worthwhile goal – an automobile'
            costing more than my house.
            The boy overshot his goal at dusk
            hit a cow on the road
            that carried no lantern
            jumped over the moon
            into a grave ready-blossoming
                —wild mustard and quack—
            the car repaired
            sold

Road boat upset
hooked as by love
the greatest thrill
since his tongue froze to the pump handle
this is the boy who'd defend you in war
and so doing crush you
haul over and love you

When other friendships are forgot
yours will still be hot

One boy there was with a camera:
'I need nests 6 or 7 feet from the ground
and on which the sun shines
most of the day. Prothonotary, please.
I'm told if anybody knows where these nests are
it will be you.'
He was a minister's son
                I never saw him—
                        driven off his course by the wind

Comes a measure marked autumn
the passing of the little summer people,
schools of leaves float downstream
past lonely piers

soft still-water twilight
morning ice on the minow bucket

Riddle me this:

                book
                brook
                        Bach
                unlock
                                ships'
                                gifts

and I'll tell you
how freedom grows.
o

2.
For Paul
Child Violinist

1
Your father to me in your eighth summer:
'Any fool can look up a term,
it's the beat and off beat, the leg lifted
or thudded that counts.'
And 'Now that I'm involved in two houses
each one a system, I realize
the less one has the richer one is
if one could sit in one spot
and write.
Paul's playing "Handel."
His eyes are clear in this air,
he sees what few others can,
the lawn is mown,
we're here till we go.'

2
Dear Paul:
the sheets of your father's book of poetry
are bound for England?
At last, after the hardships

he can say 'take back to your ship
a gift from me,
something precious, a real good thing . . .
such as a friend gives to a friend.'

You ask what kind of boats in *my* country
on my little river.

Black as those beside Troy
but sailless tar-preserve-black fish barges
and orange and Chinese-red rowboats
in which the three virtues
          knowledge, humanity, energy
infrequently ride

All children begin with the life of the mind—
if there were no marsh or stream
imagine it
99 children go into business
                selling angleworms,
the hundredth develops free fingers in John Sebastian Brook

3
Paul
        when the leaves
                fall

from their stems
        that lie thick
                on the walk

in the light
        of the full note
                the moon

playing
        to leaves
                when they leave

the little
        thin things
                Paul

4
        "Oh ivy green
      oh ivy green—"

you spoke your poem
as we walked a city terrace
and said if you could hear—sneeze
        sneeze on the corner—
                Handel clean
Christmas would be green
Christmas would be cherished.

                To the mother
        ivy
does not matter
with her son's cold no better
unless a friend should hold her
        warm in a green
                cover
then Christmas would be cherished
Christmas would be cherished.

5
They live a cool distance
inside today's woods.
My cutting friends' concise art
—intelligence in beauty—

        exacts their violinist son
        to make it come clean-sung.

Their further woods—
they live without food-heavy table,
soft bed, the whole easy lot of us,
the sick, thick leaf-tickling outersurface
lot of us.

        A tough game, art,
        humanity's other part.
o

_____

3.

Dear Paul:
the sheets of your father's book of poetry
are bound for England.
At last, after the hardships
he can say 'take back to your ship
a gift from me,
something precious, a real good thing . . .
such as a friend gives to a friend.'

You ask what kind of boats in *my* country
on my little river.

Black as those beside Troy
but sailless tar-preserve-black fish barges
and orange and Chinese-red rowboats
in which the three virtues
                    knowledge, humanity, energy
Sometimes ride.

All children begin with the life of the mind—
          if there were no marsh or stream
imagine it
99 children go into business
          selling angleworms,
the hundredth develops free fingers in John Sebastian
     Brook.

"Paul's playing 'Handle'.
His eyes are clear in this air,
he sees what few others can,
the lawn is mown,
we're here till we go."

Yes, comes a measure marked Autumn
the passing of the little summer people,
schools of leaves float downstream
past lonely piers

soft still-water twilight,
morning ice on the minnow bucket.
o

4.

Dear Paul:
the sheets of your father's book of poetry
are bound for England.
At last, after the hardships

he can say 'take back to your ship
a gift from me,
something precious, a real good thing . . .
such as a friend gives to a friend.'

You ask what kind of boats
on my little river.
Black as those beside Troy
but sailless tar-preserve-black fish barges

and orange and Chinese-red rowboats
in which the three virtues
knowledge, humanity, energy
sometimes ride.
o

For Paul: Six Alternative Sequences
Group One

I

Dear Paul
now six years old:
this book of birds I loved
I give to you.
I thought now maybe Paul
growing taller than cattails
around Duck Pond
between the river and the Sound
will keep this book intact,
fly back to it each summer

maybe Paul
o

II

What bird would light
in a moving tree,
the tree I carry
for privacy?

Down in the grass
the question's inept:
sora's eyes . . .
stillness steps.
o

III

Nearly landless and on the way to water
I push through marsh.
I lost a view . . . I saw
(and proceed in depth in place of lateral range)
the child with bigger, stiller eyes than sora's
who'd asked the carpenter, "Homer,
did you write that book?"

Yes, Paul dear, Homer's wandering through hell.
And we can't afford to hire him.
He loses ground servicing cabins—
outdoor knicknacks—that block a view.
He himself and his wife demand more elephants
on glass shelves than we have books.
People like us, child, see through it.

In summer silence moves.
Fall pheasants' cry:
rifle–shells–in–tin–box–rattle,
over us wax-leaf poplars shine and shudder
like my mother,
continue after the mind is blown.
o

IV

Understand me, dead is nothing
whereas here we want each other,
silence, time to be alone
and Paul's growing up—
baseball, jabber, running off to neighbors
and back into the Iliad—"Do you really believe
there were gods, all that hooey?"
And his violin—improvising
made a Vivaldi sequence his,
better than I could have done with poetry
at twice his age.
So writes your father, L. before P.

A start in life for Paul.
The efforts of a life
hold together as Einstein's
and lead to expectations of form.

To know, to love . . . if we knew nothing,
Baruch the blessed said, would we exist?
For Paul then at six and a half
a half scholarship—
turn the radio dead—
tho your teacher's gone back to Italy
stumped by American capital.

In my mind, the child said,
are rondeau-gavottes 1 to 11,
here is no. 12.
o

V

How bright you'll find young people,
                    Diddle,
                                    and how unkind.
When a boy appears with a book
they cry "Who's the young Einstein?"
Einstein, you know, said space
is what it's made up of.
And as to the human race
"Why do you deeply oppose its passing"
you'll find men asking
the man with the nebular hair
                    and the fiddle.
o

VI

If he is of constant depth
if he has the feeling—
numbers plus the good in 'em—
all the technique by the time he's twelve

I want that chord, you say,
and the sun and moon and stars

so what . . .
boy, are you Greek
without the Wisecrack god
o

VII

The young ones go away to school
come home to moon
like Frederick the Great
what was it he ate
that had to be sown
in the dark of the moon

Isn't it funny
how people run their acres without a hat
figuring rain in the next moon change

while you on a stool
at numbers in a heavenly scale
know the moon changes
                    night and noon
o

VIII

Some have chimes
three long things
as you come in.

They smile
and give you lettuce
because you've brought
your violin.
o

IX

You are far away
sweet reason

Since I saw you last, Paul,
my sight is weaker . . .

I still see—
it's the facts are thick—
thru glass:
a peace scare on Wall St.

                    . . .

O Tannenbaum
the children seem to sing
round and round
one child sings out:
atomic bomb

not all suckling
where Paul is
and check-writing
but as the queen, Elizabeth,
beside the barge that night
                    "longing
to listen . . .
Muzik is a nobl art"

Hi, Hot-and-Humid

That June she's a lush

She marsh wallows, frog bickering
moon pooling, green gripping

Fool
Keep cool
o

For Paul
Group Two

X

Not all that's heard is music. Paul, we leave
an air that for awhile was good, white cottage,
spruce . . . What if the sky is gone and they hold
the hill armed with tin cans—they're not bad kids
but fascists'—you have the world. Remember the
lovely notes, "the little O, the earth."
This thing is old and singing's new—you
just more full. Come, we'll sit with our birds
between city bricks. See! the sun hits.
o

XI

Let's play a game.
        Let's play Ask for a job.
What can you do?
        I can hammer and saw
        and feed a dog.
You'll do! Take this slip
to the department of song.
        You must ask me where I'm from.
Oh yes, you're from the country
called The Source.
        Will the nurse in your plant
        give me sweet pills?
No! We're not at war.
        One console-ation is:
        we can always play
        Ask for a job.
o

XII

Keen and lovely man moved as in a dance
to be considerate in his lighted, glass-walled
almost outdoor office. Business

---

wasn't all he knew. He knew music, art.
Had a heart. "With eyes like yours I should think
the dictaphone," or did he say the flute?

His sensitivity—it stopped you.
And the neighbors said, "She's taking lessons
on the dictaphone" as tho it were a saxophone.

He gave the job to someone else.
o

XIII

He moved in light
        to establish
the lovely
        possibility
we knew
        and let it pass
o

XIV

In the great snowfall before the bomb,
colored yule tree lights
at windows,
the only glow for contemplation
along this road

I worked the print shop
right down among 'em
the folk from whom all poetry flows
and dreadfully much else.

I was Blondie,
I carried my bundles of hog feeder price lists
by Larry the Lug,
I'd never got anywhere
because I'd never had suction,
you know: pull, favor, drag,
well-oiled protection

I heard their rehashed radio barbs—
more barbarous among hirelings
as higher-ups grow more corrupt.
But what vitality! The women hold jobs,
clean house, cook, raise children, bowl
and go to church.

What would they say if they knew
I sit for two months on six lines
of poetry?

o

XV

Lugubre for a child
but for you, little one,
life pops
            from a music box
shaped like a gun.

Watch! In some flowers
a hammer drops down
like a piano key's
            and honeybees
wear a pollen gown.

A hammer, a hummer!
A bomber in feathers!
Hummingbirds fly
            backwards—we eye
blurred propellers.

Dear fiddler: how'll you carry
a counter that sings
when man sprays
                  rays
on small whirring things?

o

XVI

Tell me a story about the last war.
All right, six lines, no child should hear more.

The Marshal of France made quite a clatter:
Dear people, I know you're too hungry to flatter.

But eat your beef-ounce from a doll's platter,
You'll think it's a roast wrapped in a batter.

Along came the bishop, his robe a tatter:
Sleep and it won't matter.
o

XVII

I'd like to tell you about a man
of a hundred years ago.
He was here when wild swans were still
afloat. Bigwigs wrote
from Boston: Thure, we must know
about the sandhill crane,
is it ever white with you and how many
eggs can you obtain?

Grandchildren played with his mounted birds.
"Imagine playing horse
with a pink flamingo! Imagine eight of us
schooled and exposed to a course
of music" as one of them now sums it up
to grandchildren of her own.
"And gathered around the first kerosene
lamp, how we shone."

For Thure the solitary tattler
opened a door
to learned birds—with their latest books—
who walked New England's shore.
One day by the old turnpike that still crosses
the marsh, down in the ditch
he found a new astor—to it he gave
his name as tho he were rich.

The trouble with war for a botanist—
he daren't drop out of the line of march
to examine a flower. What flower?
Shell-burst—observe a sky-exotic
attract a bomber-bird.

Dear little curlew
how are you on Willow St.
your ear on us pipers
who bleat?
o

XVIII

"Shut up in the woods"
he made knives and forks,
fumbled English gently,

"Now is March gone
and I have much undone . . ."

"It would be good
to hear the birds
along this shore intently

without song of gun."
o

XIX

Happy New Year
"Glorious and abundant
The cherry trees are in flower
In all the world there is nothing
Finer than brotherhood."
My friend, you were right.
Two thousand years
beyond you
I hand you this:

Trees' bloom with snow
clean sorrow
better than bitter
winter
       brotherhood

Resolved: beyond
flowering cherry trees
dissolved enmity
find summer
       brother
o

Group Three

I

High, lovely, light,
the Easter cake was beaten
electrically and eaten
down. Cousins, good night.

Child at your mountain-height—
your cello and bow for Easter—
high, lovely, light,
climb this one, tone feaster:

What eggs them on to bite
a frosted muff, to sneeze on,
sleep? To what season
are they tuned tight,
high, lovely, light?
o

II

What horror to awake at night
and in the dimness see the light.
        Time is white
        mosquitoes bite
I've spent my life doing nothing.

The thought that stings. How are you, Nothing,
sitting around with Something's wife.
        Buzz and burn
        is all I learn
I've spent my life on nothing.

I'm pillowed and padded, pale and puffing
lifting household stuffing—
        carpets, dishes
        benches, fishes
I've spent my life in nothing.
o

III

        Letter from Paul

It is yes with a lyre, ax and shovel
and snowman falling down.
This is my mother's birthday.
'Don't buy me a present' —what a sound—
        'don't
we can't afford it.' Selfish of her.
And when Mozart was five
        just plain 5
how proud his father was
      that his son had played
          every single note.
o

IV

Your father to me in your eighth summer:
'Any fool can look up a term,
it's the beat and off beat, the leg lifted
or thudded that counts.'
And 'Now that I'm involved in two houses
each one a system, I realize
the less one has the richer one is
if one could sit in one spot
and write.
PZ's playing "Handle".
His eyes are clear in this air
he sees what few others can,
the lawn is mown,
We're here till we go.'
o

V

To Paul reading books: Once
there lived a farmer, Crèvecoeur,
who tried to save his heart
from too much hurt.

Hero of vegetables,
hero of good
he learned to know every plant
in his neighborhood.

He loved Nantucket, grazing land
held in common.
Here one lawyer only found
the means to go on.

Green, prickly humanity—
men are plants whose goodness grows
out of the soil, Mr. Stinkweed
or Mrs. Rose.

Learn Crèvecoeur and learn fast
the firefly, two pairs of wings
and a third to read by
disappearing.
o

VI

Jesse James and his brother Frank
    raided, robbed and rode away.
Said Frank to the rising Teddy R:
    You're my type, you're okay.

Once on his way to a Shakespeare play
    Frank was almost caught.
The gunnin Jameses and the writn Jameses—
    two were taught and all were sought.

No killers were Frank and Jesse James,
    they was drove to it. Their folks was proud.
Let no one imagine they were bad as kids—
    brought up gentle in a bushwack crowd.
o

[VII]

May you have lumps in your mashed potatoes
    Henry and Wm.
cried to those who stood up to them in argu-
    ment and their words haven't died.

Don't melt too much into the universe
    but be as solid and dense and fixed
as you can. This is what Henry and Wm.
    said in the evening after 6:00.
o

Group Four

I

Sorrow moves in wide waves,
    it passes, lets us be.
It uses us, we use it,
    it's blind while we see.

Consciousness is illimitable,
    too good to forsake
tho what we feel be misery
    and we know will break.

Old Mother turns blue and from us,
    "Don't let my head drop to the earth.
I'm blind and deaf." Death from the heart,
    a thimble in her purse.

"It's a long day since last night.
    Give me space. I need
floors. Wash the floors, Lorine!
    Wash clothes!   Weed!"
o

II

I hear the weather
    thru the house
or is it my mother
        breathing
o

III

The shining brown steel casket—
what is its value really,
we already have a concrete vault.

'I don't know, they seem to want it.
Look at your automobiles—'
She who wheeled dirt for flowers

lay there deaf to death
                    parked
in her burnished brown motorless automobile.

She could have grown a good rutabaga
in the burial ground
                    edged by woods.

What is life
            in those woods one of her pallbearers
                    after a deer

'I like a damfool followed a deer
            wanted to see her jump a fence
never'd seen a deer jump a fence—

pretty thing
            the way she runs.'
    o

IV

Two old men
one proposed they live together
take turns cooking, washing dishes
they were both alone.
His friend: "Our way of living
is so different:
                    You spit
                    I don't spit."

    o

V

Paul, hello
     what do you know

Good-bye
         why

o

VI

I take it slow
     along the river
wild sunflowers
     over my head
the dead
     who gave me life
give me this
     our relative the air
floods
     our rich friend
silt

o

VII

Can knowledge be conveyed that isn't felt?
And if transport's the problem—
they tell me get a job and earn yourself
an automobile—I'd rather collect my parts
as I go: chairs, desk, house
and crankshaft Shakespeare.

Generator boy, Paul, love is carried
if it's held. Understanding you
my holdings extend.

o

Group Six

I

Ten O'clock
and Paul's not in bed!
He's reading Twelfth Night
all Viola said.

Drink to three, the family
around the bathroom tap.
Little Paul—Corelli,
what's that? Belly!

Wash and say good night
to variants and quarto texts,
emendations, close relations.
Let me hear good night.

o

Gun-night, said the kid next door,
hit the feathers, flatten,
tomorrow oil up your squeak box
and saw it off in Manhattan.

Who *is* this Shakespeer? Gimme a gander—
beard like a sea cook's. Rounded the Horn?
What kind of man is he? Why, of mankind.
Okay, like us, he was born.

o

II

If he's not peewee wafted
         tiny glissando
         in deep shade
or a newspaper
he'll attack exercises ever calculated
to float the ear in beauty.

o

---

65   *For Paul*

III

The slip of a girl-announcer:
Now we near
Boxtacota in D Minor
played by a boy who's terrific.

This saxy Age.
Bach, you see, is in Dakota
but don't belittle her,
she'll take you where you want to go ta.
o

IV

Now go to the party,
Master Paul Kung.
Wear your mother's ancient
imitation silk black dress,
whisk brush for beard,
your bathrobe's braid-tie
hung safety-pinned from Eton cap
turned front to back,
shoe string side burns
to hold the beard.

What you don't know,
that even yet
players come dressed
with shields and spears.
o

V

Am I real way out in space
asked Paul, then you see—
they rave to me of contests.
Compete, they say—my violin—
with tap-dance-acrobatics.
The winner plays the floor
with his feet.
o

Group Seven

I

My father said "I remember
a warm Thanksgiving Day
we shipped seine
without coats
nudged 20,000 lbs. of barged buffalo fish
thru the mouth of the river
by balmy moonlight
other times
you laid out with your hands glazed
to the nets."
o

Play those little records again
no sweeter music
than the violin.
o

II

The old man said you know they used
to make mincemeat with meat,
it's raisins now and citron—like
a house without any heat:

I'll roof my house and jump from there
to flooring costs. I'll have to buy
two doors to close two openings.
No, no more pie.
o

III

He built four houses
to keep his life.
Three got away
before he was old.

He wonders now
rocking his chair
should he have built
a boat

dipping, dipping
and sitting so.
o

IV

In Europe they grow a new bean while here
      we tie bundles of grass
with strands of itself—as my grandfolks did grain—
      against the cold blast
            around my house.

From my cousin in Maine: We've found a warm place
      (did she say in the hay?)
for the winter. Charlie sleeps late, I'm glad for his sake,
      it shortens the day
            around my house.
o

[V]

      On a row of cabins
      next my home

Instead of shaded here
birds flying through leaves
I face this loud uncovering
of griefs.

What irony that I
with views verdant like the folk
should be the one
to go.
o

For Paul
Group Eight

I

Paul
    when the leaves
        fall

from their stems
    that lie thick
        on the walk

in the light
    of the full note
        the moon

playing
    to leaves
        when whey leave

the little
    thin things
        Paul
o

II

To Aeneas who closed his piano
to dig a well thru hard clay
Chopin left notes like drops of water.
Aeneas could play

the Majorcan sickness, the boat on which pigs
were kept awake by whips,
the woman Aurore,
the narrow sand–strips.

"O Frederic, think of me digging below
the surface – we are of one pitch and flow."
o

III

In moonlight lies
    the river passing —
it's not quiet
    and it's not laughing.

I'm not young
    and I'm not free
but I've a house of my own
    by a willow tree.
o

IV

        If you were Pete
        and I played a guitar

So you're married, young man,
to a woman's rich fads —
woman and those "buy! buy!"
technicolor ads.

She needs washers and dryers
she needs bodice uplift
she needs deep-well cookers
she needs power shift.

A man works in two shops —
home at last from this grave
he finds his wife out
with another slave.

She'll sue for divorce
he'll blow his brains,
the old work-horse
free at last of his reins.

Oh that diamond–digging St. Louis
woman was a breeze—
now the gals got you trembling
before a deep freeze.
o

V

       "Oh ivy green
     oh ivy green — "
you spoke your poem
as we walked a city terrace
and said if you could hear
     — and I heard you sneeze —
       Handel clean
Christmas would be green
Christmas would be cherished.

      To the mother
   ivy
does not matter
with her son's cold
no better
    unless a friend
      should hold
her warm in a green cover
warm in a green cover.
o

Alternative Ending

[IV]

The cabin door flew open
       the woman fell out
it is not known whether
     she fell on land or sea

the man's grave
grave face

who were they

undoubtedly they knew tender moments
between sex and well-dressed courtesy —

men are tender with women
not passion–violent
when they are happy in general
and she — impossible to be grateful
without showing it

before the earth fell away
that they went out on Sunday to see.
o

[V]

My friend the black and white collie
stood at my door in the cold days
when the wolf was expected.
A silent long tail-waving moment
then I embraced her.
She lay her brown nose inside my coat.
We two unfortunate dogs.
o

[VI]

So you're married, young man,
to a woman's rich fads –
woman and those "buy! buy!"
technicolor ads.

She needs washers and dryers
she needs bodice uplift
she needs deep-well cookers
she needs power shift.

A man works in two shops —
home at last from this grave
he finds his wife out
with another slave.

Oh that diamond-digging St. Louis
woman was a breeze —
now the gals got you trembling
before a deep freeze.
o

___

[VII]

The elegant office girl
is power-rigged.

She carries her nylon hard-pointed
breast uplift
like parachutes
half-pulled.

At night collapse occurs
among new flowered rugs
replacing last year's plain,
muskrat stole,
parakeets
and deep-freeze pie.
o

[VIII]

           "Oh ivy green
       oh ivy green — "
you spoke your poem
as we walked a city terrace
and said if you could hear
               — sneeze
       sneeze on the corner —
           Handel clean
Christmas would be green
Christmas would be green

           To the mother
       color
does not matter
with her son's cold
no better
               unless
       a friend should tender
           rest and hold
her warm in a green cover
       warm in a green cover
o

The Years Go By

You have power politics, Paul,
You have "I'll call you, I'll call—"
which Indians did aptly
and more;—in the forest an Indian girl,
her washing spread out on a rock,
let a song fall.

You now see man hide behind
his ribs, loose grates, his kind
eye closed, the other one screwing
the savage sprays
of our steel woods' life-everlasting,
a filing refined.

But wait! In still wilder states
he'll be Needle That Clicks. Rays
will cause counters to sing
counter to sense
and man, the weapon, must obsolesce
as he radiates.
o

Paul
now six years old
this book of birds I loved
I give to you.
I thought now maybe Paul
growing taller than cattails
around Duck Pond
between the river and the Sound
will keep this book intact,
fly back to it each summer

maybe Paul
o

Paul
     when the leaves
        fall

from their stems
     that lie thick
        on the walk

in the light
     of the full note
        the moon

playing
     to leaves
        when they leave

the little
     thin things
        Paul
o

He was here before the wild white swans died out
and old country courtesy. Boston bigwigs wrote:
Dear Thure, tell us about the sandhill crane,
is it ever white with you . . . please send us
Solitary Tattlers' eggs. A latin scholar,
"shut up in the woods", he broke land,
made knives and forks, fumbled English gently:
"Now is March gone and I have much undone . . ."

Snow. Christine sick. There are two kinds of artists,
those who write for the people and those who write
for art's sake. Strong storm with colors. Marsh grass
over my head. Sent 500 insects to Berlin.
When the money comes from Leyden we'll buy coats
and shoes. Chopped five lengths of ash. Both hens laid.
Cleaned grain in the wind. Baby's coffin—I owe
two basswood boards . . . when the money comes from Leyden.

He saw Wilson's Phalarope, the beauty
among the waders. Grandchildren played
with his mounted birds. Imagine playing horse
with a pink flamingo, sighs one of them who now
has grandchildren of her own. And how they shone
gathered around the first kerosene lamp:
In the ditch by the old turnpike that still crosses
the marsh he found a new astor and gave it his name.

· · ·

The trouble with war for a botanist—
he daren't drop out of the line of march
to examine a flower. Or when half the world
is shell-burst, observes a sky-exotic
attract a bomber-bird.

o

Thure Kumlien

Bigwigs wrote from Boston: Thure,
we must know about the sandhill crane,
is it ever white with you
and how many eggs can you obtain?

For Thure the solitary tattler
opened a door
to learned birds with their latest books
who walked New England's shore.

One day by the old turnpike still crossing
the marsh, down in the ditch
he found a new astor – to it he gave
his name as tho he were rich.
o

Dear little curlew
how are you on Willow St.
your ear on us sandpipers
as you bleat
o

To print poems
is as costly
as to drill for pure
water.
o

Sorrow moves in wide waves,
  It passes, lets us be.
It uses us, we use it,
   it's blind while we see.

Consciousness is illimitable,
  too good to forsake
tho what we feel be misery
   and we know will break.
o

Old Mother turns blue and from us,
  "Don't let my head drop to the earth.
I'm blind and deaf." Death from the heart,
  a thimble in her purse.

"It's a long day since last night.
  Give me space. I need
floors. Wash the floors, Lorine!—
  wash clothes! Weed!"
o

What horror to awake at night
and in the dimness see the light.
       Time is white
       mosquitoes bite
I've spent my life on nothing.

The thought that stings. How are you, Nothing,
sitting around with Something's wife.
       Buzz and burn
       is all I learn
I've spent my life on nothing.

I'm pillowed and padded, pale and puffing
lifting household stuffing—
       carpets, dishes
       benches, fishes
I've spent my life in nothing.

o

Laval, Pomeret, Petain
all three came to an end.

Bourdet, Bonnet, Daladier
so did they.
They tried each other
they sold out their brother

the people of France.
Let's practice your dance.

o

Hi, Hot-and-Humid

That June she's a lush

Marshmushing, frog bickering
moon pooling, green gripping

fool
keep cool
o

Happy New Year
"Glorious and abundant
The cherry trees are in flower
In all the world there is nothing
Finer than brotherhood."

My friend, you were right.
Two thousand years
beyond you
I hand you this:

Trees' bloom with snow–
clean sorrow
better than bitter
winter
              brotherhood

Resolved: beyond
flowering cherry trees
dissolved enmity
find summer
              brother
o

Horse, hello

I too live hot before the final flash
              cavort for others' gain

We toss our shining heads
in an ever increasing standard of sweat

The mind deranged, Democritus
Who knows us, friend—
our indicator needles shot off scale—
Spinoza, Burns, Xenophanes knew us
in days when thought arose and kindly stayed—

All creatures whatsoever desire this glow
o

Energy glows at the lips—
a cigarette—
measure the man pending . . .

under him droppings
larger, whiter than owls'.
What thought burns here?

Time on his wrist,
soft wool zippered suit,
he speaks:
Got pure gold, boss,
if we clip the gopher now.
o

Woman in middle life
raises hot fears—

a few cool years after these
then who'll remember

flash to black
I gleamed?
o

We physicians watch the juices rise
                as we tend
                to bend her
toward the soft-blowing air.
Girl, personal grass,
                we saved you
                waved you
closer. Don't despise us
                if we ask
                or do not ask:
what for?
o

1937

In the picture soldiers
moving thru a field
of flowers,
Spanish reds.
The flowers of war
move cautiously
not to tread
the wild heads.

Here we last,
lilacs, vacant lots,
taxes, no work,
debts, the wind widens
the grass.

In the old house
the clocks are dead,
past dead.
o

In Europe they grow a new bean while here
        we tie bundles of grass
with strands of itself—as my grandfolks did grain—
        against the cold blast
                around my house.

From my cousin in Maine: We've found a warm place
        (did she say in the hay?)
for the winter. Charlie sleeps late, I'm glad for his sake,
        it shortens the day
                around my house.
o

European Travel
(Nazi New Order)

From Croatia my home to Moelling no pay
for our work, lay down at night without hay,
three days toward Berlin, one bread for six,
saw many die of cold and the whips.
At Bergen built roads tied to a pot,
crossed to Sweden tho one in our party was shot.
o

Depression years

My daughters left home
I was job-certified
to rake leaves
                    in New Madrid.

Now they tell me my girls
should support me again
and they're not out of debt
              from the last time they did.
o

Jesse James and his brother Frank
    raided, robbed and rode away.
Said Frank to the rising Teddy R:
    You're my type, you're okay.

Once on his way to a Shakespeare play
    Frank was almost caught.
The gunnin Jameses and the writn Jameses—
    two were taught and all were sought.

No killers were Frank and Jesse James,
    they was drove to it. Their folks was proud.
Let no one imagine they were bad as kids—
    brought up gentle in a bushwack crowd.

                    . . .

May you have lumps in your mashed potatoes
    Henry and Wm. cried
to those who stood up to them in argu-
    ment and their words haven't died.

Don't melt too much into the universe
    but be as solid and dense and fixed
as you can. This is what Henry and Wm.
    said in the evening after 6:00.
o

Keen and lovely man moved as in a dance
to be considerate in lighted, glass-walled
almost outdoor office. Business

wasn't all he knew. He knew music, art.
Had a heart. "With eyes like yours I should think
the dictaphone" or did he say the flute?

His sensitivity—it stopped you.
And the neighbors said "She's taking lessons
on the dictaphone" as tho it were a saxophone.

He gave the job to somebody else.
o

You know, he said, they used to make
mincemeat with meat,
it's raisins now and citron—like
a house without heat—

I'll roof my house and jump from there
to flooring costs. I'll have to buy
two doors to close two openings.
No, no more pie.

o

Version I

What's wrong with marriage?
Womens' rich fads.
Women and those "boy! buy!"
technicolor ads.

They need spinners and dryers
they need nylon slips
they need deep-well cookers
they need power shift.

You'll find the same man
working twice to give
all the things to his wife
she demands but why live

if you can't take time
to be home from this grave
or you do and your wife's out
with another slave.

She'll sue for divorce
he'll blow his brains,
the old work-horse
free at last of his reins.

Oh that diamond-digging St. Louis
woman was a breeze—
now the gals got you trembling
before a deep freeze.

o

Version II

What's wrong with marriage?
Womens' rich fads.
Women and those "buy! buy!"
technicolor ads.

They need spinners and dryers
they need nylon slips
they need deep-well cookers
they need power shift.

A man works two shops—
home at last from this grave
he finds his wife out
with another slave.

Oh that diamond-digging St. Louis
woman was a breeze—
now the gals got you trembling
before a deep freeze.

o

She grew where every spring
water overflows the land,
married mild Henry
and then her life was sand.

Tall, thin, took cold on her nerves,
chopped wood, kept the fire,
burned the house, helped build it again,
advance, attack, retire.

Gave birth, frail warrior — gave boat
for it was mid-spring —
to Henry's daughter who stayed
on the stream listening

to Daisy: "Hatch, patch and scratch,
that's all a woman's for
but I didn't sink, I sewed and saved
and now I'm on second floor."

o

I sit in my own house
secure,
follow winter break-up
thru window glass.
Ice cakes
glide downstream
the wild swans
of our day.

o

This is my mew
as our days in a wild-flying world
last —

be alone.
Throw it over — all fashion,
feud.

Go home where the greenbird
is — the trees where you pass
to grass.
o

I take it slow
        alone the river
wild sunflowers
        over my head
the dead
        who gave me life
give me this
        our relative the air
floods
        our rich friend
silt
o

He lived—childhood summers
        thru bare feet
then years of money's lack
        and heat

beside the river—out of flood
    came his wood, dog,
woman, lost her, daughter—
    prologue

to planting trees. He buried carp
    beneath the rose
where grass-still
    the marsh rail goes.

To bankers on high land
    he opened his wine tank.
He wished his only daughter
    to work in the bank

but he'd given her a source
    to sustain her—
a weedy speech,
    a marshy retainer.

o

I rose from marsh mud,
algae, equisetum, willows,
sweet green, noisy
birds and frogs

to see her wed in the rich
rich silence of the church,
the little white slave-girl
in her diamond fronds.

In aisle and arch
the satin secret collects.
United for life to serve
silver.   Possessed.

o

Dear Mona, Mary and all
you know as I grow older I think
of people when I was younger

I am lame and dizzy but eat
and hear from Ireland
where my mother was

There's a story in the paper
about the river in your country
how it's used and owned by the people

Television here but I can't use it
I'd go out of my head
old folks often can't

                . . .

International loneliness
is homed. Dear old uncle's
porch's people, prices, peppermints
rock him. He must reach
the hallway off the living room
by night.
o

THE ELEMENT MOTHER

I She's Dead

The branches' snow is like the cotton fluff
she wore in her aching ears. In this deaf huff
after storm shall we speak of love?

As my absent father's distrait wife
she worked for us—knew us by sight.

We know her now by the way the snow
protects the plants before they go.
o

II The Graves

You were my mother, thorn apple bush,
armed against life's raw push.
But you my father catalpa tree
stood serene as now—he refused to see
that the other woman, the hummer he shaded
          hotly cared
for his purse petals falling—
              his mind in the air.
o

III Kepler

Comets you say shoot from nothing?
In heaven's name what other
than matter can be matter's mother.
o

Bonpland

"Revolutionary palingenesis"—

his plants rode the Orinoco sheltered
while he sat in the rain.

He chopped, climbed, dug the jungle
for his beloved lost girl,
returned with botany
alone.

Rebellion-plotting Bogota
moved him—

nine years in Paraguay's dictator's
prison

— to graft a phrase.
o

I am sick with the Time's buying sickness.
The overdear oil drum now flanged to my house
serves a stove not costing as much.
I need a piano.

Then I'd sing "When to the sessions
of sweet silent thought"
true value expands
it warms.
o

The death of my poor father
leaves debts
and two small houses.

To settle this estate
a thousand fees arise—
I enrich the law.

Before my own death is certified,
recorded, final judgment
judged

taxes taxed
I shall own a book
of old Chinese poems

and binoculars
to probe the river
trees.

o

As I shook the dust
from my father's door
I saw young Aeneas
on the shore

mulling the past
—a large town
and a wartime island—
a pleasure now.

I'll wait, he said,
till a star shows
that's gone
when it snows.

o

97   *The Years Go By*

Your father to me in your eighth summer:
"Any fool can look up a term,
it's the beat and off beat, the leg lifted
or thudded that counts."
And "Now that I'm involved in two houses
each one a system, I realize
the less one has the richer one is
if one could sit in one spot
and write.
Paul's playing 'Handle'.
His eyes are clear in this air
he sees what few others can,
the lawn is mown,
we're here till we go."
o

Don't tell me property is sacred!
Things that move, yes!—
cars out riding thru the country,
how they like to rest

on me—beer cans and cellophane
on my clean-mowed grounds.
Whereas I'm quiet . . . I was born
with poor eyes and a house.
o

Wartime

I left my baby in Forest A
quivering toward light:
Keep warm, dear thing, drink from the cow—
her stillness is alive

You in the leaves sweetly growing—
survive these plants upheaved
with noise and flame, learn change
in strategy.

I think of Joe who never knew
where his baby went
and Mary heavy, peace or war,
no child, no enlightenment.

o

February almost March bites the cold.
Take down a book, wind pours in. Frozen—
the Garden of Eden—its oil, if freed, could warm
the world for 20 years and nevermind the storm.

Winter's after me—she's out
with sheets so white it hurts the eyes. Nightgown,
pillow slip blow thru my bare catalpa trees,
no objects here.

In February almost March a snow-blanket
is good manure, a tight-bound wet
to move toward May: give me lupines and a care
for her growing air.

o

Crèvecoeur

Letters from an
American Farmer (1782)

What a shame, said my mind, or something that inspired my
            mind,
that here, with no masters to bleed us
thee shouldst have employed so many years tilling the earth
and destroying so many flowers and plants
without knowing their structures and uses . . .
In a little time I became acquainted with every
            vegetable that grew in my neighborhood;
in proportion as I thought myself more learned,
            proceeded further . . .

perched within a few feet of a humming bird,
its little eyes like diamonds reflecting light on every side,
elegantly finished in all parts,
quicker than thought.

Thought: man, an animal of prey, seems
to have bloodshed implanted in his heart.
We never speak of a hero of mathematics
or a hero of the knowledge of humanity.

Men are like plants, the goodness, flavour of the fruit
comes out of the soil in which they grow;
we are nothing but what we derive from the air,
climate, government, religion, and employment.

Men of law are plants that grow in soil cultivated by the hands
            of others,
once rooted extinguish every other vegetable around.
In some provinces only they have knowledge,
as the clergy in past centuries in Europe.

In Nantucket, but one lawyer finds the means to live,
grazing land held in common.
I once saw sixteen barrels of oil boiled out of the tongue
                    of the whale.
No military here, no governors, no masters but the laws
and their civil code so light.
Happy, harmless, industrious people,
after death buried without pomp, prayers and ceremonies —
not a stone or monument erected —
their memory preserved by tradition.
I saw, indeed, several copies of Hudibras.

Astonishing how quick men learn who serve themselves.
At night the fireflies can be caught and used as a reading
                    light.

A Russian came to me, interested in plants.
Why trouble to come to this country?
Who knows, he said, what revolutions Russia and America may
                    one day bring about.

          (coda)

          Men who work for themselves learn
          fast. The firefly
          two pairs of wings and a third to read
          by

              disappearing.

o

To Paul now old enough to read:
Once a farmer Crèvecoeur
tried to save his heart
from too much hurt.

Hero of vegetables,
hero of good
he learned to know every plant
in his neighborhood.

He loved Nantucket, grazing land
held in common.
Here one lawyer only found
the means to go on.

Green, prickly humanity—
men are plants whose goodness grows
out of the soil, Mr. Stinkweed
or Mrs. Rose.

        . . .

Read Crèvecoeur and learn fast—
the firefly, two pairs of wings
and a third to read by
disappearing.
o

Brought the enemy down
as his descendents the bombs
blew up Somerset House—

staircase at least
where records go down
to Shakespeare who never ceased.
o

Look close
the senses don't get it all
a few hundred thousandths of a centimeter
in wave length and you see the mark
or you don't

Sylvashko and Robertson
shook hands hard
and the air was loaded
and after tea vodka—
"To the friendship of our countries"—
guilty of reason
matter that day
hit home
o

Are you high
with those whose bag is full—
"Get me a single"
"Good, I like to sleep close"—
or low
with those who must be jazzed
Honeypot
switchboard girl
hand 'em your line
they'll slip you more
nylons
than you can use
yes
go ahead
Lewd sings cuckoo
o

So this was I
in my framed
young aloofness
unsuspecting
          what I filled

eager to remain
a smooth blonde cool
effect of light
an undiffused good take,
          a girl
          who couldn't bake

How I wish
I had someone to give
this pretty thing to
who'd keep it—
          something of me
          would shape

          o

If I were a bird

          I'd be a dainty contained cool
          Greek figurette
          on a morning shore—
          H.D.

          I'd flitter and feed and delouse myself
          close to Williams' house
          and his kind eyes

          I'd be a never-museumed tinted glass
          breakable from the shelves of Marianne Moore.

On Stevens' fictive sibilant hibiscus flower
I'd poise myself, a cuckoo, flamingo-pink.

I'd plunge the depths with Zukofsky
and all that means—stirred earth,
cut sky, organ sounding, resounding
anew, anew.

I'd prick the sand in cunning, lean,
Cummings irony, a little drunk dead sober.
Man, that walk down the beach!

I'd sit on a quiet fence
and sing a quiet thing: sincere, sincere.
And that would be Reznikoff.

o

A student
my head always down
on the grass as I mow

I missed the cranes.
"These crayons fly
in a circle ahead"
said a tall fellow.

o

Sunday's motor cars
jar the house.
When I'm away on work–days
hear the rose-breast.
Love the night, love the night
and if on waking it rains:
little drops of rest.
o

Who was Mary Shelley?
What was her name
before she married?

She eloped with this Shelley
she rode a donkey
till the donkey had to be carried.

Mary was Frankenstein's creator
his yellow eye
before her husband was to drown

Created the monster nights
after Byron, Shelley
talked the candle down.

Who was Mary Shelley?
She read Greek, Italian
She bore a child

Who died
and yet another child
who died
o

I knew a clean man
but he was not for me.
Now I sew green aprons
over covered seats. He

wades the muddy water fishing,
falls in, dries his last pay-check
in the sun, smooths it out
in *Leaves of Grass*. He's
the one for me.
o

Violin debut

Carnegie Hall, the great musicbox—
lift the lid on the hard-working parts
of the boy whose smooth power
is saved—

his tone and more: what he's done with his life
—those two who sent the flow thru him have done—
he's been true to himself, a knife
behaved.
o

In the great snowfall before the bomb
colored yule tree lights
windows, the only glow for contemplation
along this road

I worked the print shop
right down among em
the folk from whom all poetry flows
and dreadfully much else.

I was Blondie
I carried my bundles of hog feeder price lists
down by Larry the Lug,
I'd never get anywhere
because I'd never had suction,
pull, you know, favor, drag,
well-oiled protection.

I heard their rehashed radio barbs—
more barbarous among hirelings
as higher-ups grow more corrupt.
But what vitality! The women hold jobs—
clean house, cook, raise children, bowl
and go to church.

What would they say if they knew
I sit for two months on six lines
of poetry?
o

Home
Version I

Swept my snow, Li Po,
by dawn's 40-watt moon
to the road that flies
to black office
away from home.

Tended my little oil-burning
stove as one would a cow—
she gave heat—till spring.
Now river-marsh-frog-clatter—
peace breaks out—

no fact is isolate —
grasses, heron, China, three
days of light:
Saturday, Sunday,
memory.
o

Version II

Swept snow, Li Po,
by dawn's 40-watt moon
to the road that hies to office
away from home.

Tended my brown little stove
as one would a cow—she gives heat.
Spring—marsh frog-clatter peace
                    breaks out.

o

Dead
she now lay deaf to death

She could have grown a good rutabaga
in the burial ground
        and how she'd have loved these woods

One of her pallbearers said I
        like a dumbfool followed a deer
wanted to see her jump a fence—
        never'd seen a deer jump a fence

pretty thing
        the way she runs

o

March

Bird feeder's
        snow–cap
            sliding
                    off

o

Two old men—
one proposed they live together
take turns cooking, washing dishes
they were both alone.
His friend: "Our way of living
is so different:

        you spit
        I don't spit."

o

My father said "I remember
a warm Thanksgiving Day
we shipped seine
without coats
nudged 20,000 lbs. of barged buffalo fish
thru the mouth of the river
by balmy moonlight
other times
you laid out with your hands glazed
to the nets"

o

I've been away from poetry
many months

and now I must rake leaves
with nothing blowing

between your house
and mine

o

He moved in light
        to establish

the lovely
        possibility

we knew
        and let it pass

o

**On hearing
the wood pewee**

This is my mew
        as our days last—
            be alone

Throw it over—
    all fashions
        feud

Go home where the green bird is—
    the trees where you pass
        to grass

o

Shut up in woods
he made knives and forks
fumbled English gently:

Now is March gone
and I have much undone

It would be good
to hear the birds
along this shore intently

without song of gun

o

To Aeneas who closed his piano
to dig a well thru hard clay
Chopin left notes like drops of water.
Aeneas could play

---

the Majorcan sickness, the boat on which pigs
were kept awake by whips
the woman Aurore
the narrow sand-strips.

"O Frederic, think of me digging below
the surface—we are of one pitch and flow."
o

Chimney Sweep

He fished the black deep
to eat,
swam the river, struck a stone
before he could sleep.

One Sunday morning,
unlearned in all but soot,
he flashed and went down
in a book.
o

I lost you to water, summer
when the young girls swim,
to the hot shore
to little peet-tweet-
                pert girls.

Now it's cold your bright knock
—Orion's with his dog after him—
at my door, boy
on a winter
                    wave ride.
o

Birds' mating-fight
feathers floating down
offspring started
toward the ground
o

T. E. Lawrence

How impossible it is
to be alone
the one thing humanity
   has never really
moved towards
o

I don't know what wave he's on
if he'll be slowed.
Once was one extended his hand.
I've lived on a bigger river—
I present a load.

o

Version I

Yes, my Time's waste.
My future ready to be filled, waits.

If this costly cold can
flanged to my house for flowing oil
to a stove not costing as much
were piano

I'd sing, dear friend,
that thirtieth: "When to the sessions
of sweet silent thought"
"sorrows end".

o

Version II

If I were buying a little piano
instead of an oil drum
—more dollars for this cold can
than bought my stove—

I'd sing, dear friend,
that thirtieth tune "When to the sessions
of sweet silent thought"
"sorrows end."

o

In Exchange for Haiku

Hear
where her snow-grave is
the *You*
        ah you
of mourning doves

o

How white the gulls
in grey weather
        Soon April
        the little
yellows

o

New-sawed
clean-smelling house
sweet cedar pink
        flesh tint
I love you

o

Popcorn-can cover
screwed to the wall
over a hole
     so the cold
can't mouse in
o

Beautiful girl—
pushes food onto her fork
with her fingers—
     will throw the switches
of deadly rockets?
o

Lights, lifts
parts nicely opposed
this white
       lice lithe
pink bird
o

If only my friend
would return
and remove the leaves
        from my eaves
troughs

o

O late fall
marsh—
                I
raped by the dry
weed stalk

o

Springtime's wide
water-
                yield
but the field
will return

o

July—waxwings
on the berries
have dyed red
            the dead
branch

o

People, people—
ten dead ducks' feathers
on beer-can litter . . .
                Winter
will change all that

o

The soil is poor
water scarce
    the people clothed
            in wind and cold—
Bolivia

o

Michelangelo

If matches had been my work
instead of marble poems
       —sulphur—
  I'd suffer
less

o

Fog-thick morning—
I see only
where I now walk.   I carry
        my clarity
with me.

o

Van Gogh could see
twenty-seven varieties
   of black
     in cap-
italism.

o

No matter where you are
you are alone
and in danger—well
            to hell
with it.
o

White
among the green pads—
      which
            a dead fish
or a lily?
o

Cricket-song—
what's in The Times—
      your name!
            Fame
here

on my doorstep
—an evening seedy
      quiet thing.
            It rings
a little.
o

Musical Toys
for a blind child

Do you see?—
sharp spires—
you could be hurt
     by the church.
Better

this dog
tinkling
     three nice
          mice
blind.
o

I fear this war
will be long and painful
and who
        pursue
it
o

In spring when the small fish spawn
goes a boat along shore—
someone scything grass?
        Slippery
Man.
o

Home/World

My life is hung up
in the flood
    a wave-blurred
        portrait

Don't fall in love
with this face—
    it no longer exists
        in water
            we cannot fish

o

Easter

A robin stood by my porch
    and side-eyed
        raised up
           a worm

o

Get a load
    of April's
        fabulous

frog rattle—
    lowland freight cars
        in the night

o

Property is poverty
I've foreclosed.
I own again

these walls thin
as the back
of my writing tablet.

And more:
all who live here—
card table to eat on,

broken bed—
sacrifice for less
than art.
o

Now in one year
          a book published
                and plumbing—
took a lifetime
          to weep
                a deep
                     trickle
o

Dusk

he's spearing from a boat—

How slippery is man
        in spring
                when the small fish
                        spawn
o

Something in the water
like a flower
will devour

water

flower
o

River-marsh-drowse
and in flood
        moonlight
                gives sight
of no land

———————

They fish, a man
takes his wife to town
with his rowboat's 10-horse
        ships his voice
to the herons

Sure they drink
—full foamy folk—
        till asleep
    The place is asleep
on one leg in the weeds
o

Letter from Ian

Aye sure
a castle on a rock
in the middle of Edinburgh

They floodlight it—
big show up there
with pipe bands
and all

Down here along the road
open your door
to a posse of poets
o

Easter Greeting

I suppose there is nothing
so good as human
immediacy

I do not speak loosely
of handshake
      which is

      of the mind
or lilies—stand closer—
smell

o

Come In

      Glen Ellyn

Education, kindness
live here
whose dog does not impose
    her long nose
and barks quietly.

Serious wags its tail
—they see us—
from curtain tie-backs
   no knick-knacks
between us.

o

---

133   *Home/World*

H. T.

Being driven after the hearse thru suburbs—
    the dead man who had been good
    and by a coincidence my father-in-law,
I sped by shop signs:
    Handel, Butcher, Shelley, Plumber
a beautiful day, blue wintry sky
such is this world.

o

The wild and wavy event
now chintz at the window

was revolution . . .
Adams

to Miss Abigail Smith:
You have faults

You hang your head down
like a bulrush

you read, you write, you think
but I drink Madeira

to you
and you cross your Leggs

while sitting.
(Later:)

How are the children?
If in danger run to the woods.

Evergreen o evergreen
how faithful are your branches

o

Linnaeus in Lapland

Nothing worth noting
except an Andromeda
with quadrangular shoots—
            the boots
of the people

wet inside: they must swim
to church thru the floods
or be taxed—the blossoms
            from the bosoms
of the leaves

o

Club 26

Our talk, our books
riled the shore like bullheads
at the roots of the luscious
large water lily

Then we entered the lily
built white on a red carpet

the circular quiet
cool bar

glass stems to caress

We stayed till the stamens trembled
o

Art Center

Glass
and wide seaview

Race that walks
            from there
you are lovely

You have *seen*
o

In Leonardo's light
we questioned

the sun does not love
My hat

attained
the weight falls

I am at rest
You too

hold a doctorate
in Warmth

o

The men leave the car
to bring us green-white lilies
        by woods
These men are our woods
yet I grieve

I'm swamp
as against a large pine-spread—
his clear No marriage
        no marriage
friend

o

Bird singing
ringing yellow
    green

My friend made green
         ring
—his painting—

   grass
the sweet bird
flew in
o

As praiseworthy

The power of breathing (Epictetus)
while we sleep.   Add:
to move the parts of the body
without sound

and to float
on a smooth green stream
in a silent boat
o

Watching dancers on skates

Ten thousand women
    and I
        the only one
            in boots

Life's dance:
    they meet
      he holds her leg
          up
o

My mother saw the green tree toad
on the window sill
her first one
since she was young.
We saw it breathe

and swell up round.
My youth is no sure sign
I'll find this kind of thing
tho it does sing.
Let's take it in

I said so grandmother can see
but she could not
it changed to brown
and town
changed us, too.
o

As I paint the street

I melt the houses
to point up the turreted cupola
I make hoopla

of the low tavern's neon cross—
very like a cross from here—
I honor the huge blue distant dome
valid somehow to the fellow falling high
o

Some float off on chocolate bars
and some on drink

Harmless, happy, soft of heart

This bottle may breed
a new race
                no war
                and let birds live

Myself, I gripped my melting container
the night I heard the wild
wet rat, muskrat
grind his frogs and mice
the other side of a thin door
in the flood

o

Poet's work

Grandfather
  advised me:
      Learn a trade

I learned
  to sit at desk
      and condense

No layoff
  from this
      condensery

o

To my pres-
sure pump

I've been free
      with less
         and clean
I plumbed for principles

Now I'm jet-bound
by faucet shower
heater valve
ring seal   service

cost to my little
  humming
     water
       bird
o

The Badlands

        Adlai Steven-
        son's death

We'd have danced
to sandstone spooks
in a beige land

but for stratified
    vacancy
o

Chicory flower
on campus

Open–field
　blue–wheeled
　　　gone by hot noon

to revolve
　earth–evolved
　　　mind–city
o

Florida

I

Always north of him
I see

his close proximity
to orange, flower

roseate bird
soft air

the state
I'm in
o

2

Henry James

St. Augustine—
they overplayed
its Spanish story
yet was this romance
that most solicited
him
o

3

Cape Canaveral

Space shot off
man appears normal
o

4

Flocks
of headkerchiefs

the pink flamingo
gone

the vanity of women
slacked
o

City Talk

I

The flower beds
          on the superhighways—
Well they have all
          the facilities
the information
          from the colleges
they force it
          and all that garbage
o

II

I'm good for people?—
penetrating?—if you mean

I'm rotting here—
I'm an alewife

the fish the seagull
has no taste for

I die along the shore
and send a bad smell in
o

They've lost their leaves
the maples along the river
but the weeping willow still
          hangs green

and the old cracked boat-hulk
    mud-sunk
grows weeds

year after year
o

Sky
in my favor

to fly
to downtown crowds
home

and Bashō
on my mind
o

Nothing to speak of
on the bus ride
—a cleaned-up route—

till the courthouse—
on that grey structure the noise
of a thousand raspy wires—

sparrows!
by what law do the chirp-screech
'sparrow folk' go screwy
the late daylight hours
of fall?
o

I visit
the graves

Great grandfather
under wild flowers, sons'
sons here—now I
      eye
of us all

but sonless
  see no
        hop
clover boy to stop
before me
o

To my small
electric pump

To sense
and sound
this world

look to
your snifter
valve

take oil
and hum
o

To foreclose
or not
on property
and prose

or care a kite
if the p-p
be yellow, black
or white
o

Scythe

Spite
     spit
loud
       sound:
where is my scy'?

Why
by your nose—
          so close
   a snake
would've bit

o

Alcoholic dream
that ran him
          out from home
               to return

leaning

like the house
in this old part
   of town leaves him
          grieving:

Why

do I hurt you
whom I love?
     Your ear
          is cold!—here,

drink

o

Consider at the outset:
to be thin for thought
or thick cream blossomy

Many things are better
flavored with bacon

Sweet Life, My love:
didn't you ever try
this delicacy—the marrow
in the bone?

And don't be afraid
to pour wine over cabbage
o

Santayana's

For heaven's sake, dear Cory,
I don't know poetry?—
I like somewhat the putrid Petrarch
And the miserable Milton
I don't have books
don't meet important persons
only an occasional stray student
or an old Boston lady.
o

Frog noise
suddenly stops

Listen!
They turned off
    their lights
o

In the transcendence
of convalescence
the translation
of Bashō
o

So he said
on radio

I have to fly
wit Venus arms
I found fishing
to Greece
then back to Univers of Wis
where they got stront. 90
to determ if same marble
as my arms
o

The radio talk this morning
was of obliterating
the world

I notice fruit flies rise
from the rind
of the recommended
melon
o

LZ's

As you know mind
aint what attracts me
nor the wingspread
of Renaissance man
but what was sensed
by them guys
and their minds still carry
the sensing
o

War

The trees full of snipers, the new kind
            of bird
Men on the hunt for Russian furs
        for Ukrainian sausage
                and Chinese girls

They floated past a crescent moon
            to Sicily—
strings of diminished pearls
            in each pearl-parachute
                a tommy gun

The Russian—only a man from Georgia
            USSR
could dance like that
            My baby son?—in some
                secret zone

o

            March

Bird feeder's
      snow-cap
            sliding
                    off

o

If only my friend
would return
and remove the leaves
      from my eaves
troughs

o

Alone

a still state hard
as sard

then again whisper-talk
preserved in chalk

At last no (TV) gun
no more coats than one

no hair lightener
Sweetheart of the whiter

walls
o

Alliance

Hunger
    with wonder

Mites wintering
    in rabbits' ears

Pronuba
    with yucca

Bashō's
    backwater

moon-pull
    He was full

at the port
    of Tsuruga
o

Churchill's Death

I was painting the
Whooping Crane, the
fingers-flying-pinnae
when the news came

Air Minister
Sir Bird–White

man-high
yard-long stride

over
and out
o

The Funeral

Out of the great courtyard
past the Tower that can be seen
        on a winter day

the Tramp of Time
via Telstar
so that we may go
                with him
o

The park
"a darling walk
for the mind"

A sense
of starlings musing
on robins

Green statue—
          Burns!

near abandoned
steepled
railroad station

lakeshore silence

glass box mushroom
with stairway stem
art museum

and townward
              the taverns
o

Swedenborg

Well he saw man created according
to the motion of the elements. He located
the soul: in the blood. Retired
at last—to a house where he paid
window-tax (for increasing the light!).
Lived simply. Gardened. Saw visions.

Nothing for supper but tea.
Now he saw the soul from his "Pray,
what is matter" leave for the touchy
—heavens!—blue rose kind of thing.
Strange—he did grow a blue rose,
you know.

o

Young in Fall I said: the birds
are at their highest thoughts
of leaving

Middle life said nothing—
grounded
to a livelihood

Old age—a high gabbling gathering
before goodbye
of all we know

o

Spring
   stood there
      all body

Head
   blown off
      (war)

showed up
    downstream

October
   is the head
     of spring

Birch, sumac
   before
      the blast

o

North Central

Lake Superior

In every part of every living thing
is stuff that once was rock

In blood the minerals
of the rock
o

Iron the common element of earth
in rocks and freighters

Sault Sainte Marie—big boats
coal-black and iron-ore-red
topped with what white castlework

The waters working together
        internationally
Gulls playing both sides
o

Radisson:
'a laborinth of pleasure'
this world of the Lake

Long hair, long gun

Fingernails pulled out
by Mohawks
o

**(The long
canoes)**

'Birch Bark
   and white Seder
      for the ribs'
o

Through all this granite land
the sign of the cross

Beauty: impurities in the rock
o

And at the blue ice superior spot
priest-robed Marquette grazed
azoic rock, hornblende granite
basalt the common dark
in all the Earth

And his bones of such is coral
raised up out of his grave
were sunned and birch–bark–floated
to the straits
o

Joliet

Entered the Mississippi
Found there the paddlebill catfish
come down from The Age of Fishes

At Hudson Bay he conversed in latin
with an Englishman

To Labrador and back to vanish
His funeral gratis—he'd played
Quebec's Cathedral organ
so many winters
o

Ruby of corundum
lapis lazuli
from changing limestone
glow–apricot red–brown
carnelian sard

Greek named
Exodus-antique
kicked up in America's
Northwest
you have been in my mind
between my toes
agate
o

Wild pigeon

Did not man
        maimed by no
                stone-fall

mash the cobalt
        and carnelian
                    of that bird

o

Schoolcraft left the Soo—canoes
US pennants, masts, sails
chanting canoemen, barge
soldiers—for Minnesota

Their South Shore journey
            as if Life's—
The Chocolate River
            The Laughing Fish
and The River of the Dead

Passed peaks of volcanic thrust
Hornblende in massed granite
Wave-cut Cambrian rock
painted by soluble mineral oxides
wave-washed and the rains
did their work and a green
running as from copper

Sea-roaring caverns—
Chippewas threw deermeat
to the savage maws
'*Voyageurs* crossed themselves
tossed a twist of tobacco in'

o

Inland then
beside the great granite
gneiss and the schists

to the redolent pondy lakes'
lilies, flag and Indian reed
'through which we successfully
                    passed'
o

The smooth black stone
I picked up in the truc source park
          the leaf beside it
once was stone

Why should we hurry
          home
o

I'm sorry to have missed
          Sand Lake
My dear one tells me
          we did not
We watched a gopher there
o

Traces of Living Things

Museum

Having met the protozoic
   Vorticellae
         here is man
Leafing towards you
  in this dark
      deciduous hall

o

Far reach
     of sand
        A man

bends to inspect
    a shell
        Himself

part coral
    and mud
        clam

o

TV

See it explained—
compound interest
and the compound eye
    of the insect

---

the wave-line
on shell, sand, wall
and forehead of the one
        who speaks
o

We are what the seas
have made us

longingly immense

the very veery
on the fence
o

What cause have you
to run my wreathed
rose words
off

you weed
you pea-blossom weed
in a folk
field
o

Laundromat

Casual, sudsy
social love
at the tubs

After all, ecstasy
can't be constant
o

Hospital Kitchen

Return
the night women's
gravy

to the cleaned
stove
o

Unsurpassed in beauty
this autumn day

The secretary of defence
knew precisely what

the undersecretary of state
was talking about
o

Human bean
and love–over–the–fence

just up
from swamp trouble
o

High class human
got no illumine

how a ten cent plant
winds aslant

around a post
Man, history's host

to trembles
in the tendrils

I'm a fool
can't take it cool
o

Stone
and that hard
contact—
the human

On the mossed
massed quartz
on which spruce
grew dense

I met him
We were thick
We said good-bye
on The Passing Years
River
o

Version I

The eye
of the leaf
into leaf
and all parts
        spine
into spine
neverending
        head
to see

leaf feather
fin fugue
modify-
renewed

union of two
in love—we—
with the same
sure thing
        to end
when one sees
new truething
Love
o

Version II

The eye
of the leaf
into leaf
and all parts
     spine
into spine
neverending
     head
to see
o

For best work
you ought to put forth
   some effort
      to stand
in north woods
among birch
o

Smile
    to see the lake
      lay
   the still sky
And
    out for an easy
      make
   the dragonfly
o

Fall

We must pull
the curtains—
we haven't any
leaves
o

Years
   hearing and sight
      passing

walk
   to the Point—
      (between the waters)

—how live
   (with daughters?)
      at the end
o

Tradition

I

The chemist creates
    the brazen
    approximation:
Life
    Thy will be done
    Sun
o

II

Time to garden
    before I
    die—
to meet
    my compost maker
    the caretaker
of the cemetery
o

To whom
can I leave
    Audubon's Avocet
    on green sportsman's cloth
    wide oak framed
    above the warm polished
    copper-braced sweet-smelling
    cedar box
when I must leave
this flyway
o

Wild strawberries
Ruskin's consolation

His grey diaries
instanced with Rose

Liver here tonight
Tomorrow we dine out

tho not like him
at Club metaphysical
o

T. E. Lawrence

How impossible it is
to be alone
the one thing humanity
    has never really
moved towards
o

Margaret Fuller

She carried books
and chrysanthemums
to Boston
into a cold storm
o

Autumn Night

Lisp and wisp
of dry leaves
'Put me wise
to what a tree toad is'
Boy

whose little son
now walks
'Starless night'
brings to mind the stars
those glimmering talks
o

Ah your face
but it's whether
you can keep me warm
o

Sewing a dress

The need
these closed-in days

to move before you
smooth-draped
and color-elated

in a favorable wind
o

I married

in the world's black night
for warmth
        if not repose.
        At the close—
someone.

I hid with him
from the long range guns.
        We lay leg
        in the cupboard, head
in closet.

A slit of light
at no bird dawn—
        Untaught
        I thought
he drank

too much.
I say
        I married
        and lived unburied.
I thought—
o

J. F. Kennedy after
the Bay of Pigs

To stand up—

black–marked tulip
not snapped by the storm

'I've been duped by the experts'

—and walk
the South Lawn
o

Alone

a still state hard
as sard

then again whisper-talk
preserved in chalk

At last no (TV) gun
no more coats than one

no higher lightener
Sweetheart of the whiter

walls
o

Why can't I be happy
in my sorrow

my drinking man
today

my quiet
tomorrow
o

And what you liked
or did—
no matter

once the moon
dipped down
and fish rose
from under
o

Mergansers
        fans
                on their heads

Thoughts, things
        fold, unfold
                above the river beds
o

Cleaned all surfaces
and behind all solids
and righted leaning things

Considered then, becurtained
the metaphysics
of flight from housecleanings
o

"Shelter"

Holed damp
cellar-black beyond
the main atrocities
my sense of property's
adrift

Not burned we sweat—
we sink to water Death
(your hand!—
this was land)
disowns
o

You see here
the influence
of inference

Moon on rippled
stream

'Except as
and unless'
o

Your erudition
the elegant flower
of which

my blue chicory
at scrub end
of campus ditch

illuminates
o

My life
　by water—
　　Hear

spring's
　first frog
　　or board

out on the cold
　ground
　　giving

Muskrats
  gnawing
    doors

to wild green
  arts and letters
    Rabbits

raided
  my lettuce
    One boat

two—
  pointed toward
    my shore

thru birdstart
  wingdrip
    weed-drift

of the soft
  and serious—
    Water
o

I walked
on New Year's Day

beside the trees
my father now gone planted

evenly following
the road

Each spoke:
Peace
o

———————

WINTERGREEN RIDGE

Where the arrows
    of the road signs
        lead us:

Life is natural
    in the evolution
        of matter

Nothing supra-rock
    about it
        simply

butterflies
    are quicker
        than rock

Man
    lives hard
        on this stone perch

by sea
    imagines
        durable works

in creation here
    as in the center
        of the world

let's say
    of art
        We climb

the limestone cliffs
    my skirt dragging
        an inch below

the knee
    the style before
        the last

the last the least
    to see
        Norway

or 'half of Sussex
    and almost all
        of Surrey'

Crete perhaps
    and further:
        'Every creature

better alive
    than dead,
        men and moose

and pine trees'
    We are gauks
        lusting

after wild orchids
    Wait! What's this?—
        sign:

Flowers
    loveliest
        where they grow

Love them enjoy them
    and leave them so
        Let's go!

Evolution's wild ones
    saved
        continuous life

thru change
    from Time Began
        Northland's

unpainted barns
    fish and boats
        now this—

flowering ridge
    the second one back
        from the lighthouse

Who saved it?—
    Women
        of good wild stock

stood stolid
    before machines
        they stopped bulldozers

cold
    We want it for all time
        they said

and here it is—
    horsetails
        club mosses

stayed alive
    after dinosaurs
        died

Found:
    laurel in muskeg
        linnaeus' twinflower

Andromeda
    Cisandra of the bog
        pearl-flowered

Lady's tresses
    insect–eating
        pitcher plant

Bedeviled little Drosera
    of the sundews
        deadly

in sphagnum moss
    sticks out its sticky
        (Darwin tested)

———

tentacled leaf
        toward a fly
                half an inch away

engulfs it
        Just the touch
                of a gnat on a filament

stimulates leaf-plasma
        secretes a sticky
                clear liquid

the better to eat you
        my dear
                digests cartilage

and tooth enamel
        (DHL spoke of blood
                in a green growing thing

in Italy was it?)
        They do it with glue
                these plants

Lady's slippers' glue
        and electric threads
                smack the sweets-seeker

on the head
        with pollinia
                The bee

befuddled
        the door behind him
                closed he must

go out at the rear
        the load on him
                for the next

flower
        The women saved
                a pretty thing: Truth:

'a good to the heart'
      It all comes down
            to the family

'We have a lovely
      finite parentage—
            mineral

vegetable
      animal'
            Nearby dark wood—

I suddenly heard
      the cry
            my mother's

where the light
      pissed past
            the pistillate cone

How she loved
      closed gentians
            she herself

so closed
      and in this to us peace
            the stabbing

pen
      friend did it
            close to the heart

pierced the woods
      red
            (autumn?)

Sometimes it's a pleasure
      to grieve
            or dump

the leaves most brilliant
      as do trees
            when they've no need

---

of an overload
    of cellulose
        for a cool while

Nobody, nothing
    ever gave me
        greater thing

than time
    unless light
        and silence

which if intense
    makes sound
        Unaffected

by man
    thin to nothing lichens
        grind with their acid

granite to sand
    These may survive
        the grand blow-up—

the bomb
    When visited
        by the poet

from Newcastle on Tyne
    I neglected to ask
        what wild plants

have you there
    how dark
        how inconsiderate

of me
    Well I see at this point
        no pelting of police

with flowers
    no uprooted gaywings
        bishop's cup

------

white bunchberry
    under aspens
        pipsissewa

(wintergreen)
    grass of parnassus
        See beyond—

ferns
    algae
        water lilies

Scent
    the simple
        the perfect

order
    of that flower
        water lily

I see no space-rocket
    launched here
        no mind-changing

acids eaten
    one sort manufactured
        as easily as gin

in a bathtub
    Do feel however
        in liver and head

as we drive
    toward cities
        the change

in church architecture—
    now it's either a hood
        for a roof

pulled down to the ground
    and below
        or a factory-long body

crawled out from a rise
    of black dinosaur-necked
        blower-beaked

smokestack—
    steeple
        Murder in the Cathedral's

proportions
    Do we go to church
        No use

discussing heaven
    HJ's father long ago
        pronounced human affairs

gone to hell
    Great God—
        what men desire!—

the scientist: a full set
    of fishes
        the desire to know

Another: to talk beat
    act cool
        release   la'go

So far out of flowers
    human parts found
        wrapped in newspaper

left at the church
    near College Avenue
        More news: the war

which 'cannot be stopped'
    ragweed pollen
        sneezeweed

whose other name
    Ambrosia
        goes for a community

Ahead—home town
    second shift steamfitter
        ran arms out

as tho to fly
    dived to concrete
        from loading dock

lost his head
    Pigeons
        (I miss the gulls)

mourn the loss
    of people
        no wild bird does

It rained
    mud squash
        willow leaves

in the eaves
    Old sunflower
        you bowed

to no one
    but Great Storm
        of Equinox

Harpsichord
& Salt Fish

THOMAS JEFFERSON

I

My wife is ill!
And I sit
            waiting
for a quorum
o

II

Fast ride
his horse collapsed
Now *he* saddled walked

Borrowed a farmer's
unbroken colt
To Richmond

Richmond How stop—
Arnold's redcoats
there
o

III

Elk Hill destroyed—
Cornwallis
carried off 30 slaves

Jefferson:
Were it to give them freedom
he'd have done right
o

IV

Latin and Greek
my tools
to understand
humanity

I rode horse
away from a monarch
to an enchanting
philosophy
o

V
The South of France

Roman temple
'simple and sublime'

Maria Cosway
    harpist
on his mind

white column
and arch
o

VI

To daughter Patsy: Read—
read Livy

No person full of work
was ever hysterical

Know music, history
dancing

(I calculate 14 to 1
in marriage
she will draw
a blockhead)

Science also
Patsy
o

VII

Agreed with Adams:
send spermaceti oil to Portugal
for their church candles

(light enough to banish mysteries?:
three are one and one is three
and yet the one not three
and the three not one)

and send salt fish
U.S. salt fish preferred
above all other
o

VIII

Jefferson of Patrick Henry
backwoods fiddler statesman:

'He spoke as Homer wrote'
Henry eyed our minister at Paris—

the Bill of Rights hassle—
'he remembers . . .

in splendor and dissipation
he thinks yet of bills of rights'
o

IX

True, French frills and lace
for Jefferson, sword and belt

but follow the Court to Fontainebleau
he could not—

house rent would have left him
nothing to eat

       . . .

He bowed to everyone he met
and talked with arms folded

He could be trimmed
by a two-month migraine

and yet
       stand up
o

X

Dear Polly:
I said No—no frost

in Virginia—the strawberries
were safe

I'd have heard—I'm in that kind
of correspondence

with a young daughter—
if they were not

Now I must retract
I shrink from it
o

XI

Political honors
         'splendid torments'
'If one could establish
         an absolute power
of silence over oneself'   .

When I set out for Monticello
      (my grandchildren
         will they know me?)
How are my young
         chestnut trees—
o

XII

Hamilton and the bankers
would make my country Carthage

I am abandoning the rich—
their dinner parties—

I shall eat my simlins
with the class of science

or not at all
Next year the last of labors

among conflicting parties
Then my family

we shall sow our cabbages
together
o

XIII

Delicious flower
of the acacia

or rather

Mimosa Nilotica
from Mr. Lomax
o

XIV

Polly Jefferson, 8, had crossed
to father and sister in Paris

by way of London—Abigail
embraced her—Adams said

'in all my life I never saw
more charming child'

Death of Polly, 25,
Monticello
o

XV

My harpsichord
my alabaster vase
and bridle bit
bound for Alexandria
Virginia

The good sea weather
of retirement
The drift and suck
and die-down of life
but there is land
o

XVI

These were my passions:
Monticello and the villa-temples
I passed on to carpenters
bricklayers what I knew

and to an Italian sculptor
how to turn a volute
on a pillar

You may approach the campus rotunda
from lower to upper terrace
Cicero had levels
o

XVII

John Adams' eyes
          dimming
Tom Jefferson's rheumatism
               cantering
o

XVIII

Ah soon must Monticello be lost
         to debts
    and Jefferson himself
              to death
o

XIX

Mind leaving, let body leave
Let dome live, spherical dome
and colonnade

Martha (Patsy) stay
'The Committee of Safety
must be warned'

Stay youth—Anne and Ellen
all my books, the bantams
and the seeds of the senega root

o

THE BALLAD OF BASIL

They sank the sea
    All land
        enemy

He saw his boats stand
    and he
        off the floor

of that cold jail
    (would not fight
        their war)

sailed anyway
    Villon went along
        Chomei

Dante
    and the Persian
        Firdusi—

rigging
    for his own
        singing

o

WILDERNESS

You are the man
You are my other country
and I find it hard going

You are the prickly pear
You are the sudden violent storm

the torrent to raise the river
to float the wounded doe

o

CONSIDER

the alliance—
ships and plants

The take-for-granted bloom
of our roadsides
  Queen Anne's Lace
  Black Eyed Susans
   rode the sea

'Specimens graciously passed
between warring fleets'

And when an old boat rots ashore
itself once living plant
    it sprouts

o

OTHERWISE

Gerard Manley Hopkins

Dear friend: If the poem
is printed few
will read and fewer scan it
much less understand it
To be sure

the scanning's plain
but who will veer
from the usual stamp and pound
Other work?—I've not yet found
the oak leaves' law . . .

o

NURSERY RHYME

As I nurse my pump

The greatest plumber
        in all the town
from Montgomery Ward
rode a Cadillac carriage
        by marriage
and visited my pump

A sensitive pump
        said he
that has at times a proper
        balance
    of water, air
and poetry

o

THREE AMERICANS

John Adams is our man
but delicate beauty
touched the other one—

an architect
and a woman artist
walked beside Jefferson

Abigail
(long face horse-name)
cheesemaker

chicken raiser
wrote letters that John
and TJ could savour
o

POEMS AT THE PORTHOLE

Blue and white
china cups
glacier-adjacent

lost
in the foothills
o

The soil is poor
water scarce
        the people clothed
                in wind and cold—
Bolivia
o

Michelangelo

If matches had been my work
instead of marble poems
            —sulphur—
      I'd suffer
less
o

Wallace Stevens

What you say about the early
yellow springtime is also something
worth sticking to
o

The man of law
            on the uses
                        of grief

The poet
            on the law
                  of the oak leaf
o

Not all harsh sounds displease—
Yellowhead blackbirds cough
      through reeds and fronds
as through pronged bronze
o

SUBLIMINAL

Sleep's dream
the nerve-flash in the blood

The sense
of what's seen

'I took cold
on my nerves'—my mother

tall, tormented
darkinfested
•

Waded, watched, warbled
learned to write on slate
with chalk from an ancient sea

If I could float my tentacles
through the deep . . .
pulsate an invisible glow
•

Illustrated night clock's
            constellations
and the booming
                    star-ticks

Soon I rise
        to give the universe
                my flicks
•

Honest
      Solid
          The lip
  of tipped
lily

A quiet flock
      of words
        not the hound-
  howl
holed
•

Night
      the sag
         of day

My mother
      all the years
          no day
o

LZ

He walked—loped—the bridge
Saluted Peck Slip
—his friend shipped fish—
     My dish

Test

and the short verse
Now he stops for lilacs
—in the *sun's* fame
     he'd say—

Stops?

Even for death
                    Z
after all that "*A*"
would dip his wool beret
to carp-fed roots

o

PEACE

Dark road home
            from town—
young neighbor as he walked
        wound up tiny Swiss works—
                    a firefly music

Mickey Mouse leaned on a bubble
            removed a tear
from the elephant's eye
        to a brush so he
                    could scrubble

Our small boat's motor raced
            Great Blue
the heron sailing as in China
        not caring
                    to win

o

THOMAS JEFFERSON INSIDE

Winter when no flower

The Congress away from home

Love is the great good use
one person makes of another
(Daughter Polly of the strawberry
                    letter)

Frogs sing—then of a sudden
all their lights go out

The country moves toward violets
                    and aconites
o

FORECLOSURE

Tell em to take my bare walls down
my cement abutments
their parties thereof
and clause of claws

Leave me the land
Scratch out: the land

May prose and property both die out
and leave me peace
o

HIS CARPETS FLOWERED
William Morris

I

—how we're carpet-making
by the river
a long dream to unroll
and somehow time to pole
a boat

I designed a carpet today—
dogtooth violets
and spoke to a full hall
now that the gall
of our society's

corruption stains throughout
Dear Janey I am tossed
by many things
If the change would bring
better art

but if it would not?
O to be home to sail the flood
I'm possessed
and do possess
Employer

of labor, true—
to get done
the work of the hand . . .
I'd be a rich man
had I yielded

on a few points of principle
Item sabots
blouse—
I work in the dye-house
myself

Good sport dyeing
tapestry wool
I like the indigo vats
I'm drawing patterns so fast
Last night

in sleep I drew a sausage—
somehow I had to eat it first
Colorful shores—mouse ear . . .
horse-mint . . . The Strawberry Thief
our new chintz
o

II

Yeats saw the betterment of the workers
by religion—slow in any case
as the drying of the moon
He was not understood—
I rang the bell

for him to sit down
Yeats left the lecture circuit
yet he could say: no one
so well loved
as Morris
o

III

Entered new waters
Studied Icelandic
At home last minute signs
to post:
Vetch

grows here—Please do not mow
We saw it—Iceland—the end
of the world rising out of the sea—
cliffs, caves like 13th century
illuminations

---

of hell-mouths
Rain squalls through moonlight
Cold wet
is so damned wet
Iceland's

black sand
Stone buntings'
fly-up-dispersion
Sea-pink and campion a Persian
carpet
o

DARWIN

I

His holy
      slowly
            mulled over
   matter

not all 'delirium
      of delight'
            as were the forests
   of Brazil

'Species are not
      (it is like confessing
            a murder)
   immutable'

He was often becalmed
      in this Port Desire by illness
            or rested from species
   at billiard table

As to Man
    'I believe Man . . .
        in the same predicament
  with other animals'
o

II

Cordilleras to climb—Andean
    peaks 'tossed about
      like the crust
  of a broken pie'

Icy wind
    Higher, harder
      Chileans advised eat onions
  for shortness of breath

Heavy on him:
    Andes miners carried up
      great loads—not allowed
  to stop for breath

Fossil bones near Santa Fe
    Spider-bite-scauld
      Fever
  Tended by an old woman

'Dear Susan . . .
    I am ravenous
      for the sound
  of the pianoforte'
o

III

FitzRoy blinked—
    sea-shells on mountain tops!
      The laws of change
  rode the seas

---

without the good captain
    who could not concede
        land could rise from the sea
  until—before his eyes

earthquake—
    Talcahuana Bay drained out—
      all-water wall
  up from the ocean

—six seconds—
    demolished the town
        The will of God?
  Let us pray

And now the Galapagos Islands—
    hideous black lava
      The shore so hot
  it burned their feet

through their boots
    Reptile life
        Melville here later
  said the chief sound was a hiss

A thousand turtle monsters
    drive together to the water
        Blood-bright crabs hunt ticks
  on lizards' backs

Flightless cormorants
    Cold-sea creatures—
      penguins, seals
  here in tropical waters

Hell for FitzRoy
    but for Darwin Paradise Puzzle
      with the jig-saw gists
  beginning to fit
o

IV

Years . . . balancing
    probabilities
        I am ill, he said
and books are slow work

Studied pigeons
    barnacles, earthworms
        Extracted seeds
  from bird dung

Brought home Drosera—
    saw insects trapped
        by its tentacles—the fact
that a plant should secrete

an acid acutely akin
    to the digestive fluid
        of an animal!   Years
till he published

He wrote Lyell: Don't forget
    to send me the carcass
        of your half-bred African cat
  should it die

  o

V

I remember, he said
    those tropical nights at sea—
        we sat and talked
  on the booms

Tierra del Fuego's
    shining glaciers translucent
        blue clear down
  (almost) to the indigo sea

(By the way Carlyle
        thought it most ridiculous
                anyone should care
        whether a glacier

moved a little quicker
        or a little slower
                or moved at all)
        Darwin

sailed out
        of Good Success Bay
                to carcass-
        conclusions—

the universe
        not built by brute force
                but designed by laws
        The details left

to the working of chance
        'Let each man hope
                and believe
        what he can'
o

PAEAN TO PLACE

            And the place
            was water

Fish
        fowl
                flood
        Water lily mud
My life

in the leaves and on water
My mother and I
                    born
in swale and swamp and sworn
to water
o

My father
thru marsh fog
      sculled down
            from high ground
saw her face

at the organ
bore the weight of lake water
      and the cold—
he seined for carp to be sold
that their daughter

might go high
on land
      to learn
Saw his wife turn
deaf

and away
She
      who knew boats
            and ropes
no longer played
o

She helped him string out nets
for tarring
      And she could shoot
            He was cool
to the man

who stole his minnows
by night and next day offered
        to sell them back
            He brought in a sack
of dandelion greens

if no flood
No oranges—none at hand
        No marsh marigolds
                where the water rose
He kept us afloat
o

I mourn her not hearing canvasbacks
their blast-off rise
        from the water
                Not hearing sora
rail's sweet

spoon-tapped waterglass-
descending scale-
        tear-drop-tittle
                Did she giggle
as a girl?
o

His skiff skimmed
the coiled celery now gone
        from these streams
                due to carp
He knew duckweed

fall-migrates
toward Mud Lake bottom
        Knew what lay
                under leaf decay
and on pickerelweeds

before summer hum
To be counted on:
     new leaves
         new dead
leaves
o

He could not
—like water bugs—
     stride surface tension
         He netted
loneliness

As to his bright new car
my mother—her house
     next his—averred:
         A hummingbird
can't haul
o

Anchored here
in the rise and sink
     of life—
         middle years' nights
he sat

beside his shoes
rocking his chair
     Roped not 'looped
         in the loop
of her hair'
o

I grew in green
slide and slant
     of shore and shade
         Child-time—wade
thru weeds

Maples to swing from
Pewee-glissando
          sublime
                    slime-
song
               . . .
Grew riding the river
Books
          at home-pier
               Shelley could steer
as he read
o

I was the solitary plover
a pencil
          for a wing-bone
From the secret notes
I must tilt

upon the pressure
execute and adjust
          In us sea-air rhythm
'We live by the urgent wave
of the verse'
o

Seven-year molt
for the solitary bird
          and so young
Seven years the one
dress

for town once a week
One for home
          faded blue-striped
as she piped
her cry
o

Dancing grounds
my people had none
    woodcocks had—
    backland–
air around

Solemnities
such as what flower
    to take
    to grandfather's grave
unless

water lilies—
he who'd bowed his head
    to grass as he mowed
    Iris now grows
on fill

for the two
and for him
    where they lie
    How much less am I
in the dark than they?
o

Effort lay in us
before religions
    at pond bottom
      All things move toward
the light

except those
that freely work down
    to oceans' black depths
      In us an impulse tests
the unknown
o

River rising—flood
Now melt and leave home
     Return—broom wet
       naturally wet
Under

soak-heavy rug
water bugs hatched—
   no snake in the house
     Where were they?—
she

who knew how to clean up
after floods
   he who bailed boats, houses
     Water endows us
with buckled floors

You with sea water running
in your veins sit down in water
   Expect the long-stemmed blue
      speedwell to renew
itself
o

O my floating life
Do not save love
   for things
     Throw *things*
to the flood

ruined
by the flood
   Leave the new unbought—
     all one in the end—
water

I possessed
the high word:
   The boy my friend
     played his violin
in the great hall
o

On this stream
my moonnight memory
     washed of hardships
       maneuvers barges
thru the mouth

of the river
They fished in beauty
    It was not always so
      In Fishes
red Mars

rising
rides the sloughs and sluices
  of my mind
     with the persons
on the edge
o

JEFFERSON AND ADAMS

1

Jefferson: I was confident
the French Revolution would end well
Adams differed: What is freedom
to their thousands upon thousands
who cannot read or write—
impracticable as for the Elephants Lions
Tigers Panthers Wolves and Bears
in the Royal Menagerie of Versailles
Our minister at Paris: Lafayette
gave dinner at my house ten days before
the fall of the Bastille
The argument at table *disfigured*
by no tinsel—cool
as Xenophon Plato Cicero
o

2

Adams to the unexploding projectile
from the forest of Virginia: *Where was you—*
Jefferson said Dear friend, I was Stoic-trained
but longed for Tranquility—
Monticello, Horace, Epicurus
I value the passions
(the senses stimulate the mind)
though yours drew you away from me
Friend Acrid to his friend Jefferson:
—no doubt you was fast asleep
in philosophical Tranquility
when ten thousand People paraded
the streets of Philadelphia
o

PROTHONOTARY WARBLER

Version I

Clerk of May Court
singing ringing
yellow green

St. Francis image
as perch—why judge—
a niche in the wall

and the man made green ring
in his painting—grass
the sweet bird flew in

and the friend took it
to testify: (Willa)
"they know how to live"
o

Version II

Bird singing
ringing yellow
        green

My friend made green
            ring
—his painting—
        grass
the sweet bird
flew in
o

WARBLER

St. Francis' image
        —no grimace—
looks down
        past the nest in the niche
        and the yellow green
                sound

It is right
        to delight
in this ringing
            bird-light
            from the emerald
                    ground
o

KATHARINE ANNE

            A poor poet
            divining Gail

The baby looked toward me
and I was born—
to sound, light
lift, life
beyond my life

She wiggles her toe
I grow
I go to school to her
and she to me
and to Bonnie
o

SEASON'S GREETINGS

      card

Thomas Jefferson, manufacturer of nails
         and passionate architect.

For austere education, the Stoics, for
         tranquility
of mind, the Epicureans and for love of
fellow men and charity, Jesus
o

Jefferson—statesman
   Hopkins—poet
      on the uses
         of grief

Hopkins
    Jefferson
      on the law
         of the oak leaf
o

Everybody's nose's full
of spray—the air's full
of all those bottles of stink
pffing out in mist. My Sin
Evening in Paris

Taboo, Wind Song—
every girl and her feller
they spray it on the air
they spray it on their hair
when they go off.

o

In the hills
for a few days
couldn't write

Gone further found
less—maybe
you know the place.

o

BASHŌ

beholds the moon
       in the water

He is full

at the port
       of Tsuruga

o

from THOMAS JEFFERSON

My wife is ill!
And I sit
            waiting
for a quorum
o

from DARWIN

His holy
            slowly
                        mulled over
        matter

OTHER WRITING
Radio Plays
Creative Prose
Three Reviews

Radio Plays

The President of The Holding Company

PRESIDENT:
I will enforce it that after supper you speak about dusk.

SECRETARY:
I have this concrete immolence

VOICE OUTSIDE:
this messenger from the dead.

PRESIDENT:
Have you looked up Sumatra's defence of cat-tails?

SECRETARY:
Pardon sir, who gives you fanatic worry when the rest of us boop
on the stairs?

PRESIDENT:
I consume it my dignity

VOICE OUTSIDE:
to go straight to the devil

PRESIDENT:
Stuff and retain him . . . I'll have him by the stem of his hat.

SECRETARY:
O Matchbox, save him, he's the best timidity we have.

PRESIDENT:
O why am I tired why haven't I
a circumlocus of design
someone to come in and say
the pears smell ripe here . .

But I'm bound to the fears of my weathers.
Are you ready to release the evening?

SECRETARY:
Maygo is waving his voice by the well.

PRESIDENT:
Success like raisins comes first in the mouth.
But who wants a mouthful of raisins.

VOICES OUTSIDE:
Sylva Wergles was a worty witchwoo
She lived by the side of a tree.
She combed the worldside for pennies and peas
And wood a few sallies to sea.

---

233   *Radio Plays*

O my, said the counterfeit judge, By the boo
You cost me a tendril and then a long shoot.
Get thee from me and relate
How frogs come out of a gate.

SECRETARY:
? It can't be commercial poetry.

PRESIDENT:
I doubt its prowess. It lacks compulsion.

VOICES OUTSIDE:
O sweet little Tilda's an open sale
She comes from a baudy and lands in a gale.
She tunes up the strings of her gay rig-a-roo
And plays a high banner to how so come who.

PRESIDENT:
The traffic is ended. The last star is a bonded issue. Sighing is
extinct. I've gone to the morning entry.

o

Fancy Another Day Gone

The glare from the brass horn makes sun-brown satin fit smoothly the girl by the window. Even the young man is straight and bright.

HE:
Please come. I want you to justify my landscape.
(She looks out of the window and lights the late afternoon.)

HE:
I love you magnificently. I've had every drop of
blood from the moonstone put into a venture for you.

SHE:
(takes his hands) It's a high hurt.

HE:
The plight of the individual is our happy finale.
(Both absorbed by the glow move out.)

GRANDMOTHER:
(sidling the luminous flood) She picks and promises and castillates the dew. And he's a tin whistle substitute, works for the wonder constructor who eats and then expectorates when he wants to build a lake where a hill is.
The family, entering, pales and points after tea-time.

MOTHER:
Studying? Why so stupid, son.

STUDY BOY:
(in khaki) They're putting us thru an elemental dog-trot in sargonic culture. We're now at the hammer and fan-wheel stage,—star-falling comes next.

MOTHER:
And this painting, daughter, that you hold so dear . .

FATHER:
A silk contortion heavily blotched toward the centre.

DAUGHTER:
He has issued also complaints in vast design.

BLUE TIE SON:
The very devil of a good thought.

GRANDMOTHER:
He ate a mushroom for breakfast. He can't be divine anymore.

MOTHER:
He wears that kind of practitioner's overcoat . .

BLUE TIE:
He repeatedly assumes his dais.

FATHER:
All the same, I'd write him and ask what his inventions are.

DAUGHTER:
He's done a great deal with words that look like pictures.

FATHER:
I don't suppose a father ever cocktailed his hopes to that.
(chorus by two small children skipping in and out):I don't suppose a man ever, no, I don't suppose a man ever.

MOTHER:
What unbooked revelry . .

GRANDMOTHER:
Today let us weep for tomorrow may be frought with foolishness.

MOTHER:
(pauses in front of daughter before going off completely) Darling, you've some bad laughter lines.

DAUGHTER:
But facts are a mass of coercives.
(Children dance in to tea-table and away.)

GRANDMOTHER:
Not a raisin goes to cookie in this house but what they know it.

STUDY BOY:
(The room grows an even, late daylight—Study boy takes his books nearer the window.) This map has a cherry expedition punctured by tooth-picks to rescind a felled hatred. Wind me a furlough. I'm bound to need air.

SLEEPY SON:
Feathering Heights—how they can dance up there.

BLUE TIE:
And let their seams out in the wind . . .

SLEEPY:
Sweet pillow, Madge. What exquisite tether and release. A little difficult, tho, to be a constant wind.

STUDY BOY:
Oh you don't use the right weapons.
(small children and Grandmother sing out):

> "Rings on your fingers,
>   bells on your toes,"
> Tether your feathers,
> Tar all your foes . .

DAUGHTER:
Flightful conceit. . . .

GRANDMOTHER:
Somnambule enchants a wiry daisy, curvets and comes back.

STUDY BOY:
I prefer my women on paper.

BLUE TIE:
(looking into cup) Concatenations streaking a bird with a tail-light.

SLEEPY:
Hang your tea-cup relations.

BLUE TIE:
(idling about the room, glances over father's shoulder at magazine) Literate man would like to hear from readers interested in talking about things that count.

STUDY BOY:
What's a dismissed attavater?

BLUE TIE:
It means the ease comes out of the sound.

FATHER:
It's what is called imminent custody.
(piano fortissimo from a nearby key)

DAUGHTER:
Beethoven's ironworks. *(The room is a strong dusk and the window steel-blue)*
(pianoworks)

STUDY BOY:
Don't invert me. I wasn't so smelted in a long time.
(Piano fades along with the family, the Octaves of Point Lessening.) Tomes at the window establish the smoke scene as the night of the mandolin query.

HE:
Vertebrate lives spread the hour. On the instable count no face line ever vented approach.

SHE:
Is the midnight capsule ready to gloat?

HE:
It's only lachrymose and octo-even by the enervator on the tombstone. Fentry the watchman restored his eyesight on that.

SHE:
These failings tie you up with home. For me it's just unknown distance.

HE:
My dear, I care a great deal for the pear-shaped of the lute species.

SHE:
It's hard to glutinize in leafless time.

HE:
Who has unsettled you about this matter?

SHE:
Oh—appetizers, upholders of the law . .

HE:
Drizzlers in the sink.

SHE:
My faint memory of viscera should be certainly viscarra. Let's rush the blood to some other point.

HE:
I suppose it's profound to guess whether . .

SHE:
(plucks the mandolin) Prayerful inebriate shelters his wings.

HE:
(blows his cigarette smoke white in the dark) I shall never be able to enlarge my scope as I wish.

SHE:
Have you been to the proper authorities?

HE:
Don't be nemeebic.

SHE:

I love you despite the coconut on your tie.

HE:

Would you be traditional in buttering your bread?

SHE:

Not if there were plums to placate the ardor.

HE:

Then what are we waiting for?

(Grandmother candles her hopes to an empty room, has them blown by the wind at the window, trudges the length of the night.)

Domestic and Unavoidable

Voices from dining room and hall off study. Voices of old man and old woman as their shadows pass to and from dining room near entrance of study—they carry trays of food and drink; their forms are reflected on wall of study. The curtain rises on a young man seated at desk in the study, busy with pencil, paper and ruler. The only light is shed from a shaded lamp down onto desk so as to leave the rest of room in comparative darkness. A confused murmur of voices of men and women from dining room becomes merely a suspicion of sound as of air in a tunnel or as a loud speaker of a radio turned on but not speaking—movement in stillness out of which the action of the words comes clear.

Gentleman gentle	: . . . .*Miserly.* . . .
Woman high	: . . . .*motion.* . . .
Woman low	: . . . .*intensifies a goal.* . . .
Gentleman loud	: . . . .*and a featherman's.* . . .
Woman husky	: . . . .*hat*
Old man	: (with bottle and spoon*) Take every hour when necessary; the complaint must be necessary several hours.*

Gentleman gentle	: . . . .*Ex-.* . . .
Gentleman loud	: . . . .*collect.* . . .
Woman high	: . . . .*in trinity.* . . .
Woman low	: . . . .*and doubly the canticle.* . . .
Woman husky	: . . . .*waste.*
Old man	: *They don't have a minister, they have a doctor.*
Woman husky	: *Oh do you think we should indoctrinate at certain points?*
Gentleman loud	: *Well, one thing.* . . .
Woman low	: . . . .*announces a fabricoid.* . . .
Woman high	: . . . .*and another.* . . .
Gentleman gentle	: . . . .*assembles a divinity.*
Gentleman loud	: . . . .*Downstairs I tender the right.* . . .
Old woman	: *After dinner the women smoke and the man retire to the front room.*
Woman high	: *Some men, they say, entered the forest to-day; it was a bad omen; not long after a tree fell.*
Young man in study	: *Will they come in scarlet or in the month of the first canterbury bells?*
Woman low	: *Have you been.* . . .
Woman high	: *To the bread-eaters' lately?*
Young man in study	: *Marigolds in stink-orange.*
Old woman	: *I suppose if they need stones she'll have to go along; they'll want time to pay for 'em.*
Young man	: *Always through windows a curtain about somebody else.* (He gets up to look through curtains, heavy curtains as for a doorway, but whether there is a window or doorway the audience cannot tell)
Woman low	: (Near) *When I'm alone it's an open day. I clouded myself on him.*
Woman husky	: *But surely there is another who scenes passably?*
Woman low	: (Nearer) *Night that opens its puny residua unoccupied of sleep.*
Young man	: (Now back at desk, looks up quickly towards curtains, is silent) (All "sound" ceases. There is now and while young girl and young man are to talk normal quiet and absolute quiet. Girl's voice (she is never seen) is close and intimate)

Young girl plain	: *Garden plans? I couldn't pre-arrange a garden. I'd hate to come upon a flower and find I'd put it there.*
Young man	: *Who are you?*
Young girl	: *O. S. R. Return.*
Young man	: *Only scientists have three initials and a last name.*
Young girl	: *My hand scratches seeds of whorfels.*
Young man	: *She's unconscious. It must be her strong will that does it.*
Young girl	: *And corners are precarious beasts. They put a wall of weeping between us, suffering, the technologic absolute.*
Young man	: (shifting in his chair) *My dear I have other affiliations. It's been penciled and ruled. My life is elsewhere.*

(Confused murmur begins off stage)

Young girl illumined	: *Oh I shouldn't want you to be faithful to me alone.* (Light in study is turned off immediately— controlled back stage. Servants' pantomime on wall again—definite)
Old man	: (Puts his arm around the old woman.)— *That's a very good mousetrap.*
Old woman	: *How comes?*

(Confused murmur becomes "sound". Light turned on in study as if by anyone unseen who finding no one there turns it off again—or merely what it is: controlled back stage)

Gentleman gentle	: *Minockua. . . .*
Woman high	: *. . . .the day is fattening. . . .*
Gentleman loud	: *. . . .Brimble. . . .*
Woman husky	: *. . . .the Brand. . . .*

(Doors close, keys jingle)

CURTAIN

o

As I Lay Dying

radio adaptation of William Faulkner's novel

DOC PEABODY (as narrator): Anse Bundren's wife Addie was dying. When Anse finally sent for me of his own accord I said: He has wore her out at last. And when it got far enough into the day for me to read weather signs I knew it couldn't have been anybody but Anse that sent. I knew that nobody but a luckless man could ever need a doctor in the face of a cyclone. And I knew that if it had finally occurred to Anse himself that he needed a doctor, it was already too late. Their cotton and corn farm lay on top a steep hill. My team couldn't make the last several yards up the steep but Anse got me up there—my 250 pounds—with the help of a rope. "What the hell does your wife mean," I say, "taking sick on top of a durn mountain?"

ANSE (thick, gentle voice): I'm right sorry, Doc.

PEABODY: Well, let's go in.

Sound of footsteps, door closing.

PEABODY (as narrator): The girl Dewey Dell was standing by the bed fanning her. Addie turns her head. She's been dead these ten days. I suppose it's having been a part of Anse for so long that she cannot even make that change, if change it be. I can remember how when I was young I believed death to be a phenomenon of the body; now I know it to be merely a function of the mind— and that of the minds of the ones who suffer the bereavement. The nihilists say it is the end, the fundamentalists, the beginning; when in reality it is no more than a single tenant or family moving out of a tenement or a town. Beneath the quilt she is no more than a bundle of sticks. I turned to Anse standing there with his arms dangling, the hair pushed and matted upon his head like a dipped rooster.

PEABODY: Why didn't you send for me sooner?

ANSE: Hit was jest one thing and then another. That ere corn me and the boys was aimin' to git up with, and Dewey Dell a-takin' such good keer of her, till I jest thought . . .

PEABODY: Damn the money. Did you ever hear of me worrying a fellow before he was ready to pay?

ANSE (low-voiced, concerned): She's goin', is she?

ANSE: I knowed it. Her mind was sot on it. She laid down on her bed. She says: I'm tired.

PEABODY: And a damn good thing.

PEABODY (as narrator): Suddenly Addie looks at me. Her eyes like lamps blazing up just before the oil is gone. She probably wants me to get out and everybody else. I've seen it before in women. Seen them drive from the room them coming with sympathy and pity, with actual help, and clinging to some trifling animal to whom they never were more than pack-horses. That's what they mean by the love that passeth understanding: that pride, that furious desire to hide that abject nakedness which we bring here with us, carry with us into operating rooms, carry stubbornly and furiously with us into the earth again.

ANSE: (kindly and close in) The boys went for another load, Ma. Them three dollars, you know. They thought you'd wait.

ADDIE (weakly but clearly): I smell wet leaves and earth (fade to background during next two speeches) geese flying north . . .

PEABODY: She seems to be talking to herself.

ANSE: I'll go out and see if them boys are coming. (door closing)

ADDIE (stronger, closer in): I was young then. I was teaching school. One day in early spring a man appeared, turning his hat round and round in his hands and I said, "If you've got any womenfolks, why in the world don't they make you get your hair cut?" He said, "I aint got none." And that was Anse and I took him. And when I knew I had my child, Cash, I knew that living was terrible and that words are no good; words don't ever fit even what they are trying to say at. We had to use each other by words but most of all by blood, blood coursing, boiling, whipping— only by something like the whip could my blood and their blood unite in one stream. I loved Anse but my aloneness was violated. When I found I had Darl I saw only one thing—Anse had tricked me. But no, I had been tricked by words older than Anse or love and the same words had tricked Anse too. And when Darl was born I asked Anse to promise to take me back to Jefferson when I died. Father had said that the reason for living was to get ready to stay dead for a long time. I knew that father had been right, even when he couldn't have known he was right any more than I could have known I was wrong. Anse was dead and didn't know it. Anse was dead (falters, weaker, then suddenly tries to raise up and call) Is Anse dead?

PEABODY: Calm yourself, Addie.

ADDIE: As I lay in the nights I heard the words that are the deeds, and the other words that are not deeds, and that are just the gaps in people's lacks, coming down like the cries of the geese out of the wild darkness. But I found it—the reason for life was the duty to the alive, to the terrible blood, the red bitter blood boiling through the land. My children were of the wild blood of me and of all that lived, of none and of all. Then I found that I had Jewel— when Jewel was two months gone. Then Dewey Dell, then Vardaman. And then I could get ready to die.

ADDIE (rather loud): Cash. You, Cash! I want the boy. (weaker): Anse, Jewel, Darl . . .

ANSE (kindly and close): They went for another load, Ma, three dollars, you know. They thought you'd wait.

PEABODY (as narrator): So she died. The child Vardaman, was somewhere about. Dewey Dell sat motionless awhile, then Anse reminded her to get supper.

ANSE: We got to keep our strength up. And Cash'll need to eat quick and get back to work so he can finish the coffin in time.

PEABODY (as narrator): I stepped out into the twilight, Dewey Dell behind me. I could feel the 17-year-old girl's big dark eyes boring a hole through my back.

DEWEY DELL (low, rich voice): I'll have to look for Vardaman. (Lower, fuller, more intimate—she always speaks from the depths but now as though to herself alone): You, Doc Peabody, could do so much for me if you just would and if you just would then I could tell you and then nobody'd have to know it except you and me and Darl and Lafe. You could help me if you would.

Sound of door

ANSE: God's will be done. (sighs) Now I can get them teeth I been needin' for so long.

DEWEY DELL (off some distance, voice raised): Vardaman. (Louder): You, Vardaman. Bring that fish for supper. Come now, right away.

VARDAMAN: (little child's voice, always tiny, distinctive, thin, "talking to himself like a cricket in the grass", Faulkner says, "a little one.") Here I am right here by the porch. Yuh, I've got a fish, my fish, hey, where's my fish? I cut his guts out but Dewey Dell wants to cut him up for supper. (Starts crying): And that man—he came and kilt my Maw. He came and kilt my Maw.

DEWEY DELL (normal voice): Stop that.

VARDAMAN (no longer crying): My mother is a fish.

PEABODY (as narrator): Yes, Addie Bundren was dead but to get her into her grave how many miles away in Jefferson where she asked to be buried with her kinfolk—that was another matter. As one of the neighbors said, "It's just like Anse to marry a woman born a day's hard ride away and have her die on him." *A day's* hard ride! With the rain falling and rivers rising up over the bridges who knows how many days.

ANSE (as if looking out over the land, rubbing his knees): No man mislikes it more than me. And me without a tooth in my head, hoping to get ahead enough to get my mouth fixed where I could eat God's own victuals as a a man should. And her hale and well as ere a woman in the land until that day, ten days ago.

PEABODY (as narrator): Jewel, Darl and Cash came home. We ate. Cash started making the box.

Sound of sawing and occasionally, nailing.

ANSE: (to Cash): I ain't much help carpentering, Cash.

CASH: Darl is here.

DARL: Next thing it'll do, Cash, is rain. Think you'll get the coffin made tonight? Here's a lantern. (To himself): It takes two people to make you, and one people to die. That's how the world is going to end. Dewey Dell wanted her to die because then she'd get to town.

DEWEY DELL (as if to herself): God gave woman a sign when something has happened bad.

DARL (to himself): Yes. Cash is nailing her up. Jewel sitting there looking disconsolate. (To Jewel): It's not your horse that's dead, Jewel.

JEWEL: Goddam you. You always were a queer one.

DARL (as narrator but as though to himself): The air smells like sulphur. Cash works on, arm bared. Below the sky sheet-lightning slumbers lightly; against it the trees, motionless, are ruffled out to the last twig, swollen, increased as tho quick with young. It begins to rain. The first harsh, sparse, swift drops rush through the leaves and across the ground in a long sigh, as though of relief from intolerable suspense. They are as big as buckshot, warm as though fired from a gun; they sweep across the lantern in a vicious hissing. From behind Pa's slack-faced astonishment he muses as though from beyond time, upon the ultimate outrage. (To Cash): The lantern's getting wet. *Sound of saw ceases.* Here, you'd better put on Mrs. Tull's raincoat. (Again as narrator): Cash hunts the saw. After awhile we find it in Pa's hand. (To Cash): Going to bevel all those boards? It'll take more time.

CASH: Yuh. The animal magnetism of a dead body makes the stress come slanting, so the seams and joints of a coffin are made on the bevel. It makes a neater job.

Sound of sawing and nailing and rain and then fade out

PEABODY (as narrator): It's almost day when Cash finishes. Four of us carry the coffin to the house. Addie could not want a better box, Cash is a good carpenter. And why not? Didn't she pick out these boards herself? Before she died, Cash brought each board to her for her approval. Darl lies down for a couple of hours.

DARL: I know. I know. In a strange room you must empty yourself for sleep. And before you are emptied for sleep, what are you. And when you are emptied for sleep you are not. And when you are filled with sleep, you never were. I don't know if I am or not. How often have I lain beneath rain on a strange roof, thinking of home.

Silence

PEABODY (as narrator): On the day of the funeral Brother Whitfield came in wet and muddy to the waist. He had swum the river on his horse. The rain washed the bridge out.

WHITFIELD: (chants): The Lord comfort this house. The Lord giveth . . . The Lord put his grace on this house. May she rest in peace. I went down to the old ford and swam my horse over, the Lord protecting me.

SEVERAL MEN (chanting): The Lord giveth. The Lord giveth. The Lord giveth . . .

NEIGHBOR (rough drawl): That ere bridge was built, let's see, in 1888. I mind it because the first man to cross it was Doc Peabody coming to my house when Jody was born.

PEABODY: If I'd crossed it every time your wife littered since it'd a been wore out long before this.

Sudden laughter at this remark as release, then sudden quiet as they real-ize indiscretion and take sidelong glances at each other.

NEIGHBOR: Only the Lord can get Addie Bundren across the river after this rain. A misdoubtful night last night with the storm mak-ing. I knowed it was an evil day when I seen that team of Pea-body's come up lathered, with the broke harness dragging and the neck-yoke betwixt the off critter's legs. Not too bad a wind but the rain. It'll take Anse a week to go to Jefferson and back. It's the cotton and corn I mind. Washed clean outen the ground it will be. A fellow wouldn't mind seeing it washed up if he could just turn on the rain himself. Who is that man can do that? Where is the colour of his eyes? Ay, the Lord made it to grow, the Lord giveth . . .

MEN CHANTING; not quite in unison: The Lord giveth. The Lord giveth. The Lord giveth . . .

PEABODY (as narrator): And the next day they should have started off. I said, "Anse, now about the wheel for the wagon, will Jewel get it fixed?"

ANSE: Jewel will git back with it, I reckon, Doc.

NEIGHBOR: Take my wagon, Anse.

ANSE: Thank yuh, but I'll wait for ourn. She'll want it so. She was ever a particular woman.

NEIGHBOR: You'll have to go way around by Samson's bridge. It'll take you a day to get there. Then you'll be 40 miles from Jefferson. Take my team and get started right away, Anse.

ANSE: We'll wait for ourn. I'm goin fishin in the slough.

NEIGHBOR: That slough aint had a fish in it never that I knowed. Aint no good day to fish anyhow.

ANSE: It's one in here. Dewey Dell seen it.

NEIGHBOR: Tell you what—let's all get started to where you're goin' and when we get to the river me and you'll take our poles and catch some fish.

ANSE: One in here. Dewey Dell seen it.

VARDAMAN: Pa shaves every day now because my mother is a fish.

Sound of wagon creaking fading in and occasionally mules snorting. Then sudden stop.

PEABODY: (as narrator) At long last the wagon was ready, the mules hitched to it. Everybody gathered in the yard ready to go.

climbs onto the wagon, her leg coming along from beneath her tightening dress: that lever which moves the world; one of that caliper which measures the length and breadth of life. She sits on the seat beside Vardaman, drops a basket of lunch in the bottom of the wagon and holds a square package on her lap.

ANSE: You, Jewel, leave that horse behind and come sit with us in the wagon. It aint respectful to your Ma to ride that horse like you wuz goin to a circus. A durn spotted critter of a horse, wilder than a catty-mount, a deliberate flouting of her and me. Her wanting us all to be in the wagon with her that sprang from her flesh and blood.

JEWEL (evenly but staunchly): I'm taking my horse.

Sound of Darl laughing.

JEWEL: I didn't laugh, that was Darl.

ANSE: How many times I got to tell you, Darl, it's laughing like that that makes folks talk about yuh. Right on the plank where she's laying.

DARL: (toning down his laughter): All right, let's go. Good-bye Doc, see you some day.

PEABODY: Good-bye, good-bye. (Lowering voice): And time, I'd say. (Wagon creaking fades in and then fades out). (As narrator): I heard the rest of the story from Darl later.

Sound of wagon creaking and mules.

DARL (as narrator): Kind of nice, the mud whispering on the wheels. And Jewel's horse moving with a light, high-kneed driving gait just back of us.

CASH: It'll be smelling in a couple of days now.

ANSE: It's a hard country on a man; it's hard. Eight miles of the sweat of the body washed up outen the Lord's earth, where the Lord himself told him to put it. Nowhere in this sinful world can a honest hard-working man profit. And the towns live off them that sweats. It's only in heaven every man will be equal and it will be taken from them that have and given to them that have not by the Lord.

CHANT OF MEN'S VOICES WHISPERING: Nowhere in this sinful world can a honest hard-working man profit. Nowhere in this sinful world . . .

VARDAMAN: There's the river, Pa, there's the river. See?

ANSE: We're gettin to Samson's at dusk-dark. How's the bridge?

DARL: Washout out, just like Tull's. No, just under in the middle, out at both ends but swaying back and forth like a grass carpet.

ANSE: We'll stay at Samson's for the night and if it dont rain cross over in the morning.

SAMSON: Howdy, folks. Unhitch your mules, Anse, and come in to supper.

ANSE: We'll stay in the barn, thank yuh, we've got something in the basket.

SAMSON'S WIFE: Look here, come on in to supper and then go to sleep in a bed. You've got to get your rest. I believe in respect for the dead but you need your sleep.

ANSE: No thank yuh, ma'm, I wouldn't be beholden.

SAMSON: The best respect you can pay her now is to get her in the ground the quickest you can. You better give up going to Jefferson, Anse, and go over here to New Hope, only three miles, bury her there.

DEWEY DELL: (with great urgency): Pa, you promised, you gotta take her to Jefferson—if you don't do it, it will be a curse on you. You promised, you've got to.

ANSE: Did I say no?

SAMSON: (lowers his voice as if to himself): Stubborn, the lot of em. Those bone-gaunted mules of theirn . . . and that girl watching me. If her eyes had a been pistols I wouldn't be talking now. (Raises his voice to speak directly to them): Well, come in later on to sleep just as my wife said.

ANSE: I thank yuh but I'll stay up with her. I don't begrudge her it.

DEWEY DELL: (to herself): I took the knife from the steaming fish and killed Darl. Darl's eyes. Because he knows.

ANSE: (to himself): Now I can get them teeth. That will be a comfort, it will.

DARL: Look up in the sky.

VARDAMAN: Buzzard.

Silence
Sound of rooster crowing. Noises of dawn. Sound of wagon creaking along.

DARL: Yes, the bridge submerged in the middle. Sagging and swaying.

Sound of wagon creaking gives over to water swirling.

CASH: Well—a fellow could walk across yonder on the planks and logs that have caught up on the ford past the jam—showing nothing under em though—might be quicksand built up there. What you think, Darl?

DARL: Let Pa, Dewey Dell and Vardaman walk across on the bridge, the water won't be too high for that. And then we'll go in the wagon over the ford best we can.

PEABODY'S VOICE (as narrator): Sure, there they were, ready to go through the water. That girl, too, with the lunch basket on one arm and that package under the other. Just going to town. Bent on it. They would risk the fire and the earth and the water and all just to eat a sack of bananas.

DARL: Jewel—

JEWEL: I'll go ahead on the horse. You can follow me in the wagon.

DARL: Right. And Jewel, take the end of the rope upstream and brace it. Will you do that, Jewel?

JEWEL: I don't give a damn. (Voice in high tension above increasing sound of water swirling and logs jamming): Just so we do something. Sitting here, not lifting a goddam hand . . .

DARL: (above the noise): The motion of the wasted world accelerates just before the final precipice. Doc Peabody, would you have gone over?

PEABODY (as narrator): An irrevocable quality. I can see it—the mules stand, their forequarters already sloped a little, their rumps high.

Sound of mules breathing with a deep groaning sound.

DARL: Jewel's horse is sinking. No, there he is again. Cash, steady the coffin. Wait—here comes a log! Cash! We're gone!

PEABODY (as narrator): I know just how it was—a log surged up out of the water and stood for an instant upright upon that surging and heaving desolation like Christ.

CASH (yelling): Darl, get out. (Frantically): Look out! Jump!

Sound of crash and destruction and animal cries. Then dead silence.

PEABODY (as narrator): The wagon, the box with the dead, Darl, Jewel, Cash's carpenter tools, Cash himself, did you think they wouldn't get out of it? Cash had a broken leg but he claimed it bothered him none. They hitched up somebody's team, laid Cash on top of Addie and here they go again.

Sound of wagon creaking along and perhaps sounds of life along the road—car passes sounding its horn, etc . . .

DEWEY DELL: Pa, I gotta stop.

ANSE: Can't you wait till we get to town—we aint got time if we want to get there by dark and get the hole dug.

DEWEY DELL: No, I gotta go in the bushes. I won't be long.

Sound of wagon ceases.

JEWEL: Taint nothing to dig a hole. Who the hell cant dig a hole.

DARL: I'll bet Dewey Dell changes clothes. Sure, there she is already. Sunday dress, beads and shoes and stockings.

ANSE: (long suffering): I thought I told her to leave them clothes to home.

DARL: (to himself): I wonder what she'll accomplish in town.

Sound of creaking of wagon fades out and city street noises fade in. Sound of footsteps and a screen door opening and closing. A small bell sound as of door or ringing of cash register.

MALE VOICE, drug store clerk: Yes ma'm?

Silence.

DRUG CLERK: Yes, ma'm?

DEWEY DELL: I want something, suh . . . can we talk private . . .

DRUG CLERK: What is your trouble?

DEWEY DELL: Well—female trouble, suh. I've got ten dollars. Lafe said I could get it at a drug store.

DRUG CLERK: But ma'm, you've come to the wrong place—

DEWEY DELL: This is a drug store, aint it? We'll never tell you sold it to us, never, suh.

DRUG CLERK: Listen, you go on home, buy yourself a marriage license with that ten dollars.

DEWEY DELL: (pleading): If you've got something, let me have it.

DRUG CLERK (to himself): It's a hard life they have, sometimes a man . . . (Raises voice and speaks directly to her): Look here, the Lord gave you what you have even if He did use the devil to do it. (Lowered voice again as if to himself): Funny looking set, that's her family out there on the street I guess, in the wagon. I heard somebody say they were running around getting cement—*cement*—for the boy's broken leg. And the wagon smells as though there was something dead in it. They'll all hole up in jail the lot of em. This girl's not bad looking, though—I might as well play along with her. (Normal voice again but with a reckless, philandering quality): Well, here's something then—

DEWEY DELL: It smells like turpentine. You sho this will work? Is this all there's to it?

DRUG CLERK: I tell you what you do. You come back at ten o'clock tonight, I'll give you the rest of it.

Silence. Then montage of voice, each as if talking to himself.

VARDAMAN: Hurry up, Dewey Dell. Hit smells.

DARL: How does your leg feel, Cash?

CASH: Fine. The stuff is cool on it.

VARDAMAN: Jewel hasn't got a horse anymore.

ANSE: I wouldn't be beholden.

CASH: It don't bother me none.

DEWEY DELL: I just know it won't work. I just know it won't.

VARDAMAN: We can sleep on the straw tonight with our legs in the moon. Jefferson is no longer a far piece.

CASH: Ah—go easy. For the sake of Christ.

Now they speak directly to each other.

PEABODY: Go easy! (Snorts): Raw cement! Don't you lie there, Cash and try to tell me you rode six days on a wagon without springs with a broken leg and it never bothered you.

CASH: It never bothered me much.

PEABODY: Raw cement! You mean it never bothered Anse much. Don't tell me. And don't tell me it aint going to bother you to have to limp around on one short leg for the balance of your life—if you walk at all again. God Amighty, why didn't Anse carry you to the nearest sawmill and stick your leg in the saw? That would have cured it. Then you all could have stuck his head into the saw and cured a whole family . . . Well, now you've got her in the ground, where is Anse, anyhow, what's he up to now?

CASH: He's taking back them spades he borrowed.

PEABODY: Of course he'd have to borrow a spade to bury his wife with. Unless he could borrow a hole in the ground. Too bad you all didn't put him in it too . . .

DARL: Here comes Pa now.

VARDAMAN: Who's she coming with him? Who's she?

CASH: Looks like the woman he borrowed the spades of.

Sound of footsteps fading in

ANSE: Young uns, meet Mrs. Bundren.

PEABODY (as narrator): And damned if he didn't have teeth too.

o

**From *Taste and Tenderness*,
a two-act play about the Jameses.**

Act I, Scene 3

William's room. He is now 30, Alice is 24.

WILLIAM: (writing in his journal at table) She's gone. A part of myself was lowered into the grave with her today. Minny— Minny Temple is dead. (Rises with gesture of futility) Death or life—it's all one meaning. What about that part of me left here to fight through this nothingness—the nothingness of this egotistical fury! William James, what about it? All the years of study—introspection—give it all up! Restrict myself to anatomy. What then?— count vertebrae for the rest of my life? I read Biblical texts to console myself these days. I *expect philosophy* to pull me out. Do I have the strength—the sheer physical and mental strength—to develop a complete conception of things? Because in the end if I want a philosophy with no humbug in it I'll have to write it myself! (Consults his watch) Harry! I wish you'd get here—the boat must have been late. I wonder if he'll know. It's so hard to forget her *life*. Minny—Harry. His stories—his characters touch us as she did—their orbits come out of space and lay themselves for a short time alongside ours, then off they whirl again into the unknown. After his year in England he'll come home healthier and happier—the only one of father's children moving into something like mental equilibrium. (Alice is at the door, enters in a silent, reflective mood, stands) Eh . . . Alice!

ALICE: I've decided to stay.

WILLIAM: Little sister—

ALICE: It wasn't—*wrong*—of me to have considered—?

WILLIAM: Who can be considered educated who hasn't thought of—of ending one's life. But you'll stay here?

ALICE: Here with good mother and poor dear old good-for-nothing papa. (Brightening) While William is at hand being William and Harry is taking possession of London as Henry James, the novelist. Yes, I'll fight the Irish cause from here!

WILLIAM: That's my old Bottled Lightning speaking—(The door is softly pushed open by Harry, overcoat on arm, hat on head and holding package and valise. Alice and William throw their arms about him and relieve him of his things.)

WILLIAM: You know?

HARRY: Minny . . . (now disengaged from his brother and sister) It's the living who die and the writers who go on living.

ALICE: Minny's death marks the end of our youth.

Darkness

o

Creative Prose

Uncle

There were three crows sat on a tree,
They were as black as crows could be;
One said to the other see
The farmer sowing his seed—
Isn't he wonderful kind to the poor
*   I'm sure.*

(from hearsay)

He loved the quiet and peace of his old country home. He was a
quiet man. But such a career he must have, my Uncle, as to keep
him making a name for himself. Changes took place in the coun-
try while he, John Julius Benjamin Beefelbein, went on making
the same name. Not aggressive—a liberal who gave and accepted
all. In the fight to win the good things of life, comfort and retire-
ment from grinding work, and in order to keep his home in the
country, Uncle Babe—Matty, fifteen years older than her brother,
called him Babe without thinking even when he was big—entered
public service at the height of which the initials J. J. did not mean
an overpowering gain.

The family, the two old folks, sturdy proprietors of the resort
hotel home, and their daughter and John, entered the fierce
struggle to get ahead. But then when I speak of the family in those
days I speak of Friedericka, the parent with the flying petticoats
sometimes rustling as of sateen, asperity in her whole manner, and
she wished she had taffeta. I knew her when I was playing around
the place as the child of her niece—we stayed there, my mother
and I, while my father was away in a sanitarium. Whereas Great-
Uncle Gotlieb, tall, happy, head thrown back . . . I thought I was
to call him *Great* Uncle because he had such great smiling wrinkles
around his eyes . . . braided my hair and told me nursery
jingles. . . . There *were* three *crows* sat *on a tree.* . . . And if he saw
me at a distance outdoors he'd hold out his arms wide. He was
too easy-going for Aunt Riecky. At this time Uncle John as a
boy—I suppose I called him Uncle because he was next in line to
Great Uncle, open, good natured—was away at school in Mil-
waukee, home only in summer. The folks were trying their best
to give him the advantages. They knew he applied himself at
books and was always busy learning to be somebody in an office.
Matty was learning to be a dressmaker in town and already sewing
for others, helping with John's expenses. Matty was a tall, lean
strong figure of a woman, sharp eyes and nose but not bad look-
ing. She often suffered from neuralgia and colds, all from having

walked a mile crosslots in woods and marsh to country school—
Gotlieb took the children on the road only when the road was
passable—and she sat through her lessons with cold feet, perhaps
wet. She was Asperity's daughter, though, and went through
everything. She could be seen at times, a large handkerchief folded
over her head and ears and tied under her chin, working on wash-
board and sewing machine. Once, I remember, after she'd
scrubbed the floor, she stood clapping her hands hard to the
words: Now my strength is all gone! She inherited the virtue of
work from her mother, as in a way did John. Inherited?—but in
those days things were stolidly saved and passed along in the fam-
ily and couldn't be changed. Riecky was the family, but I always
thought my Great Uncle Gotlieb was somebody too: he was a
naturally happy man. She scolded him for this or that—he stayed
out fishing too long and didn't catch anything or slept after the
noonday meal and beer or he dressed and cleaned the wild fowl
he'd shot so late that she had to milk the cow and feed the horse
and her blood was aroused, and this with her habit of work put
her through the chores in a hurry. She always did what was
needed, cleaning, cooking and directing. Was clean and saving and
made it go. She said Gotlieb had a poor way of making it, no
action, would never have money, but with her it was different.
She could buy their food in winter and when spring came could
have $3 left.

Many times my Uncle Gotlieb of happy actions could be seen
walking outdoors, food and drink in his belly, his gun in his hand.
Like a landlord, Riecky said, walking around on the lawn. He was
considered a good hotel man, people liked him, he enjoyed being
a proprietor. A certain class of people came out from Milwau-
kee—cheese makers and store owners who had money. But usu-
ally he was waiting for just anyone to blow in. He may have
wanted to be a policeman but outside of town there was no
chance, or game-warden, but in those days there were no laws
restricting the catch of plentiful game. He must have thought of
some princely office or just some good job whereby he might
sleep two hours after dinner and the woodbox wouldn't even have
to be filled. He sold fish and canvasback ducks to a hotel keeper
in the city and John helped with this when he could.

They were not church people—this was a resort nine miles
from the church the farmers were afraid of. They had a feeling
about wrong-doing though, knew that you always got paid for
wrong-doing, and Riecky especially knew all the orthodox sins.
Was a time in Uncle Babe's life when he believed he should be-
come a church man but he resented being preached to or thought

he should be the one talking, and it seemed two hours every week wasted when he should be attending to his business and helping people. Matty, tolerant—when another German family never let a Good Friday go by without noodles, prunes and fish—says, That's alright but I wasn't brought up to be a Christian like that.

Riecky believed in working for people who paid. If they did or especially if they didn't, she cleaned until she was aroused to a frazzle, it was her morality. She left a smell of dirty, oily rags where she'd cleaned, very rank till you got used to it. You had to go through hard things in order to get somewhere in the world, she said. She did her best to rid the place of rats, would often say they should be caught alive, taken up by their tails and dipped in tar. Matty was strong like that, rising up in her frail health.

Uncle Gotlieb worshipped as he saw fit. He said, as he stood looking up, Trees are the best things a man can have that little while he lives. He would make chests of drawers in wintertime and neat little models for boats or small launches to be built later outside if he could get the materials. You loved to pass your hand over the models, so smooth, dark-rubbed walnut; one now hangs above Matty's sewing machine.

I always thought the people were really good. What held them back was something they were laboring under—

The place . . . trees thick, great branches. Robins' nests allowed on the window sills on the store-room side of the house. Evenings the red-wings, the wind died down, the little river still. The birds gathered close in a song of settling down . . . over two hundred acres . . . owned by the family—

The moss green Morris Chair. The shadows plush green in the water. Pictures of afternoons of those days: women in their chairs, the mild, wild lowland, excessively beautiful, willows, ease-ness, drooping health, the ladies with long, flowing skirts, their handkerchiefs in their laps. The Beefelbeins on such occasions dressed not unlike the guests.

—The breaths of the women wafting over the children, perfume catarrhal or from rich eating. Sweets were honored, oranges not easy to get.

—Often nothing to do. A great deal depended on the people who came to the hotel. The Beefelbeins catered mostly to two families of cheese makers, their brothers, and friends who were store men. The two cheese makers were big people—each weighed close to 300 lbs. Withal, they were democratic, and often, Riecky thought, quite common. Their wives wore silk dresses, were refined; the entire crowd demanded good food and waiting on and no matter how sick they got from boat or beer, they always, said she, ate good. After all, they shouldn't think they were Rockefellers—there were people in the world had more money than they. She would imitate them, set two teaspoons at table even when only one was needed—for coffee, the dessert being cake. Everyone knew her, though, for a woman of few dishes. She considered herself socially superior to moneyed people—the virtue of hard work was on her side—*they* could get into trouble and lazy ways, she thought, spending for rich dishes and drink. The fact that her work served trouble and that it earned her not one-half dozen fresh pineapples or one new jacket in five years . . . she had little time to think about it.

—Sometimes on spring election days, her money spent for taxes, she would serve Uncle Gotlieb with the blitz kuchen and soup and water-cress and handcheese he loved—always the handcheese in a jar back of the stove—and she would ride with him to town over the muddy road after the long winter—he had to attend to voting, didn't he?—an important day for men and they were treated to cigars by those who were running. John had a poem in his schoolbook about voters by a man named Whittier. . . . She would make it known to Gotlieb that she wanted him to buy her a blouse and a hat, thus making herself dear to him.

—He admired her caprice; it was part of her energy and he knew which side of his life the kitchen was on. I suppose she never failed to say, several times a week, after he'd gone off with his gun and come back ready to enter: Now Pa, I've just cleaned.

—The large range she cooked over was always hot, and always she made her own butter and sausages and bread and cheese. Some of the vegetables from the garden she canned. In summer a grocery wagon would come through and she liked to patronize the man who ran it as much as she could. We must patronize him, she told Gotlieb. Sometimes she traded wild fowl or fish for coffee or sugar. The stove would go out only between dinner and supper on hot summer days. Matty now has a beautiful electric range, and beside it on her little wood-and-coal heater is an oven to save electricity. Both the old folks often said, I don't know what it's coming to.

So the big cheese makers would write to Great Uncle Gotlieb to meet them in town at the depot with the two-seater: Will be 4 of us, will make it worth while for you. And when he'd get there he'd find four beside the two big men and two kegs of beer and a barrel of cheese and other food and suit cases of luggage. Uncle would have to go twice back and forth with them and then again to leave his rented buggy and one horse and bring his own horse and small buggy home, a long day, and sitting alone on this last trip, darkness closing in, mosquitoes, he thought how long he would have to wait—two months, six months, for his money—he could have got it after a month or so, Riecky at him why he didn't, but he had his pride and wouldn't ask a dollar from anyone and he knew they would pay in full and more too whenever they got around to it.

And it wasn't long before they had him making merry with them, blowing the foam off their beer mugs *splotch* on the walls. And they pressed cheese upon him. Perhaps they liked people to whom they could be in debt and surely they liked to have people in debt to them. They took enjoyment in those who owed them something. We love you to stay this way, poor, working for us, they said, we want to be your Patrons. Postponement of the pay might even extend over into the next year but then a silk dress would accompany the big check and a silver dollar for Matty and John each. It was just their leisurely, aristocratic social-democracy, perhaps even a kind of aesthetic. They were cultured and didn't have to think of money. And my great Uncle was cultured too and couldn't demand. Really everyone accepted it as policy. The cheese people still held the mortgage on Uncle's place and although it put Gotlieb in embarrassment to have to be a little late with the interest, that's the way it was in the country. It was this confusion that kept Uncle Gotlieb doing things for them without knowing just where he was. Undoubtedly much the same thing contributed to John's later political and business decorum of letters and dinners and third persons and, as Matty said, handkerchief wavings. So as the days went on the more the Beefelbeins had to do for their boarders so as to be sure the bill would mount up to where they might sooner be paid. Meanwhile their beer would run out and Uncle could make a little profit selling them his own.

The one man paid Uncle Gotlieb or Johnny immediately upon rowing him out in the boat, and more, so as to keep them working to make it up. The other cheese man would never pay. He wanted to be rowed out onto the lake, the little river emptying into it a quarter mile down, and then rowed around in the bay, fish a little here, and a little there, the oars under the hands cracking, blistering in the hot sun. He would forget to pay, he didn't mean anything by it, he just didn't settle. Both men left the feeling with the Beefelbeins that money was the power but that it made people fat and lazy, money corrupted those who had it. Such people had it too good, Riecky said, high livers. The men sometimes sick from wine or beer had to have Gotlieb support them up the stairs to their bedrooms. I can remember seeing him half carry one of them up and Riecky's summer wurst hanging from the ceiling of the upstairs hallway.

The feeling that money was bad. Same with machines, city industries that used newer and newer machinery and threw men out of work. Money, principally, was bad.

It was a hard pull. If things had gone better, John might have continued his education in Milwaukee, this way it was broken off when he as nineteen. He came home, wondered what to do with himself. Roamed with the dog, quietly amused himself, greeted some of the old hotel guests, kept shy of new ones. He was usually a happy person like Uncle Gotlieb, looked like him, same pleasant good face, his nose more of a button, stature about the same—in fifteen years more he was to take on a plumpness making him appear bigger than his father. Plump—Matty shook her head and said he must be taking after some ancestor they'd all missed.

Often John as a boy was not to be disturbed. It seemed to him the less he did the more his mind worked. Gotlieb understood this in a way, considered the boy more refined than he was himself, educated, his world therefore a little different from that of the old stogies in the wilderness. Let him drift a bit. Johnny would take a boat, paddle out and lie in it. He would look at a tree in a certain light; his sensations the moment he looked formed the tree, he thought, and no one else would find that tree to be just what he found it, and he wondered if the song sparrow would have perched there just then if he hadn't been looking. But Riecky was watching. As John landed back on shore she said, Time for those trees to be cut, been hanging there crowded too long.

He became interested in the fyke net fishing, got together a small outfit with Gotlieb's help. When John had saved $250 he put it into a cheese factory. The man who came around had been a good talker. Wisconsin was a great dairy state, cheese factories were doing a big business. John's education cut off in his freshman year of Normal School he realized he must depend now on working with his hands and then invest his savings, depend on what money could bring as to further education and leisure. He must be able to stand up against any man. A decent supply of money was good. A decent business, a fair profit—as he looked about him he couldn't quite help coming to that conclusion so early . . . he came to it helplessly. But it may be said to his credit that he was never against most of the things money can buy. He was a man who wanted to spend money and have nice things. When a chair was without a pillow or an upholstered seat he would reach over to the sofa and get hold of one of Matty's dark red plush cushions. She would indicate he should take the little old pad that the cat used but he would wink and say, This plush is just as good. Or at table he'd butter a piece of kuchen in place of his mother's or Matty's bread maybe getting dry and hard, and with Uncle Gotlieb's smiling wrinkles acclaim buttered kuchen just as good. Riecky and Matty always held the hard view.

The way the cheese industry developed—a factory sprang up here or there in this country by itself for itself but somehow supposedly for the common good, entering the free competition against others that sprang into individual profits if lucky. Some got themselves joined to a big chain controlled possibly in New York. "Filled cheese" was produced by mixing foreign fats, animal or vegetable, with skimmilk. The original butterfat extracted, a cheaper substitute used. In some cheese was found the best cottonseed oil. Much of the full cream cheese was excellent for people who could afford it. John's factory springing up north of Milwaukee was going to produce good cheese. He hit upon putting his money into this concern and letting it work for him. It failed. A big monopoly forced out, sprung, the little one. Uncle Babe went to Milwaukee to the old cheesemaker friends to try through them to bring pressure to bear—he was always to say: find the right people and through them bring pressure to bear—but they were in the business themselves. He didn't think the men in charge of the factory were really dishonest—they had to suffer with the rest—they were making a cheese that was not "filled." New York Cream Cheese it was called. Showed they believed in honest food products.

The Beefelbeins were great cheese people, always had it in some form or other. In the years Riecky was making it at home the state was producing many thousands of pounds and always doubling the amount annually. Hers was good, they knew what went into it, they were used to it. They might have bought some that was better. And again, her sausage meat—to this day Uncle John can find no sausage meat like the old people made it in their homes—he can't think what it's made of now. And shoes—paper!

Matty, dully, when she heard of John's failure: Cheese kriste. And then went about her housework with force. The way she looked at it, it was just whether you were lucky or not. Baking, weather, business, all depended on luck.

John, well, he felt—poorer. His mind went back to the Indians, he could only believe their life was best, they had no financial troubles and they had been happy with what they had. At times during his life his mind went back like this. Isolated country living: each family attending at home to its own needs, what a man could do alone was best. Still, he couldn't worry too much now, he was young and everything was possible. You had to go through hard experiences, he guessed, before the good things of life would come. Life is a struggle. The fittest survive. . . . etc. . . . He went at it harder, fishing, always the desire to make something of himself, become a director himself. Gradually he went in deeper and hired a crew of five men. Hard work but making money.

One morning he went out to raise his nets. The game warden who had to supervise for the state, see that only carp and buffalo were taken to be sold, told Uncle John he couldn't raise nets, orders from Madison. At the same time John happened to know the permission to raise nets was given as usual to a man engaged in fishing farther down the river. Immediately he got himself a letter of introduction to the governor of the state, Uncle John, went and explained his cause: he'd paid license and was law abiding, now for no apparent reason the state would do this to him. He hinted that the other man down the river had paid more to gain favors? In ten minutes the governor cleaned out the conservation department, fired everyone who had anything to do with it and thanked Uncle John for coming—just like that.

To this governor Uncle John always felt he owed a great deal. But then if anyone at all ever did anything for him he thought about it and could never do enough for that person. He would do things all his life for the person who was kind to him. Perhaps out of this experience he saw a chance for coupling gratitude, service, with self-help. If only he could enter a political career. He fished now by seine, shipped rough fish in refrigerator cars to New York. He stood in rubber waders in ice cold water to his waist, subjected himself to rheumatism, smelled of fish slime and invested his money in carefully considered places. But politics, politics, it hemmed him in. A career . . . it would not let him rest.

Fight was in the air. The governor was a fighter, all good political men were. You had to fight the big business monopolies and the poorer you were the more fight it took. You really had to find at least one financially independent friend who could furnish money for your campaigns. It was a great game. You had to know psychology . . . he wished he knew more, had had a full college education. His idol, in that young man's last year as a student, had been chosen, after preliminary tests, to represent his school in the state collegiate oratorical contest, and had then won the prize at

Beloit with an oration on the character of Shakespeare's "Iago" and then won in the interstate meeting and all this was in the newspapers, so it was said that later when he went among the farmers he found they could place him right away. John wished he knew Shakespeare like that, culture. Throw in his lot with culture and property. He did not even know law. But if his heart was in the right place. . . . You had to know how to handle people who favored the "interests." For example, you advocated railroad taxation bills, showing the "interests" and the general public at the same time hotly that railroads could increase their rates and take back the amount lost through such taxation, so that the railroads would let the tax bills go through and the people would become aroused under higher rates and there was your regulation of rates to furnish the next campaign. Because you had to keep yourself in office. A constant fight.

Yet Uncle Babe was the quietest of men, easy-going, Matty said, and I always knew him to be gentle. I was about eleven when the cat was lying helpless under the front porch, a leg broken—my mother and I lived here almost entirely now, my father had died, the doctor said at the last he should have been in a hospital, but it was an unfortunate case, we hadn't enough money—and Uncle Babe, interested in the kitty almost as much as I was, jumped into his Cross-Country Rambler, went to town and brought back a doctor friend and the cat grew well, our Josephine who played for us in the railing of the stairway. John could never see any animal, anybody, suffer. Sometimes he would forget to do the actual work of caring for them—thinking about other things. He always preferred Matty to cut the heads off the poultry. But he took advancement in the world as hard and serious, as probably most young men who have any talent and intelligence, but mainly because of the strain of their schooling however short, the constant strain of competition, always one first above all, a few up and the neighbors down, the ratings, the contests, the shame if you stopped to think and be considerate and received no high mark, the prizes that drove to the quick; the desire to get ahead was paramount, nervous, forceful. He sincerely desired to become a leading force in political reform if he could get to champion the right group.

He would start close to home, would take up the cudgels for the farmers. The farmers' taxes were too high. They had no market close by for their livestock—did, yes, but it held the prices up—most cattle and hogs were shipped way to Chicago and then the meat was shipped way back again. There seemed to be no great farmer issue before the public, though. This governor wasn't doing so much for the farmers, in a way, yes, but he had his railroads to fight. Perhaps there was no field. But they always said they couldn't sell their produce for more than it cost them to produce it and this was wrong. What was the trouble? They weren't organized. There was a field. They should be made to see what was good for them, join together under a competent head, form a small monopoly, a farmers co-operative, demand good prices. People did not always know what they could do to better themselves till someone came along and pointed it out.

The oleomargarine fight had benefitted the farmers and the fight was still on. Grover Cleveland had said, "I venture to say that hardly a pound (oleomargarine) ever entered a poor man's home under its real name and in its real character." The packers and the Presidents, Uncle John, extended their sentiments to the poor. One must be strong. As he saw it: butterfat and beef fat both, but yes, butterfat.

The people here had a former governor to thank for what the dairy industry had become. He was a poor man but he rose to be Wisconsin's principal spokesman for the dairy interests in state and congressional hearings. He started in this very section on a farm in beet raising or was it hops and that year the market was glutted and of course he'd borrowed heavily and now his character had to stand or fall by whether he could or could not pay back, and he had failed through no fault of his own except that he was a party to a blind system. If he couldn't pay back he had no honorable character. The story is told that The Honorable Mr. Y. went into a grocery store one day, lifted a sack of flour on his back, walked out. They'd have to knock him down if they wanted it, he said, he had no money and his family had to eat. In time, however, he entered the disastrous, free competition again by way of a different business and as luck would have it bettered himself—at the cost of his neighbors though he wouldn't have meant it that way—and paid back every dollar he owed. In fact no man was a man unless he struggled under a great load against odds. Life was a struggle. This man was energetic and experimentative but he could not get ahead as he liked. What could he do not always having land and cattle and other materials to carry out his ideas? Everything connected with farming was slow. An accurate test for determining the amount of butterfat in milk had to be invented so that the creamery man would not cheat himself nor the farmer. The test finally accepted came out of the Wisconsin College of Agriculture, was received into the creamery industry with very little opposition and into the entire United States and even foreign countries. The Babcock Test can beat the Bible in making a man honest, said a cream man.

Legislators fought each other in campaigns for leadership and in offices too. One said to himself: I must fight this thing through, I know it will be worth while and so-and-so will be true to me. Among these individuals were militant liberals on all sides. Great speechmaking and handclapping . . . perhaps the people would forget their troubles. Sometimes the men were lawyers, got very much interested in making intricate cases. Was it constitutional, they asked, when people organized into strikes. Uncle John, but that was later, had to pay the processing tax on a pig before such tax was declared illegal. It was important to get the labor vote, but many times a well meaning senator or governor would be told, Oh, nevermind about the labor vote, Brown will take care of that, or Payne.

The current of thought started above and came down! Spirit, mind, existed before trees and rock?

The military spirit handed down to J. J. Beefelbein—was it for him? Could he stand it? He told himself yes. He would show 'em he could hand back just what they gave him.

He, Beefelbein, would organize the farmers.

So he started out, sometimes with horse and buggy, sometimes with the Rambler, depending on the road, and usually carried a sack or two of Red Lime Fertilizer, the agency he'd taken as an opportunity to combine salesmanship with—salesmanship! He felt if he could get them to try what he had to offer they'd never be without it.

He followed the farmers from the barn to the house and around. Not easy to gain their attention, busy plowing, milking, making hay, feeding stock, planting, cultivating—how many hours a day did a farmer work? Only time really was the noon hour and then they wanted to rest; even J. J. liked his noontime undisturbed like his father before him. They would nod to him after their heavy meals of hot soup and heaped up plates of potatoes, almost as though the radio had come already, their heads would fall from side to side on their chests as they rested in their chairs. Same way the evenings and to bed early to get up early. He managed to tell them he was organizing a farmers' co-operative. The strength of other industries lay in the power of combining and what they could do the farmers could do. When he said, We will pay the capitalists in their own coin, this did fire them. Only trouble was: they couldn't pay to enter it. And they had joined such an organization sometime before and nothing happened. He pointed out this would be bigger, more powerful, like the labor unions only better because "we" could handle "our own" products. They didn't like the mention of labor unions but John pointed out that whereas labor unions were perhaps socialistic, the farmers' union would be the good American thing. Of course, he said, no one group should be allowed to gain ascendency over others, this was democracy. He must have thought it funny that one side could never be right but he was a man who always tried to see both sides. They all probably implied: capitalism has to exist in order to have labor unions; price determines need; strikes cause confusion in industry. Price determines need! John saw through that—funny!—and he told them how they could turn it the other way around. When he had their attention—time is slower out here than in the cities, so much space, people acres apart, illusion of freedom is greater—he would put the question: would they give their support? And they would smile: there'd be big ones in it would get sumpn, not they. They seemed better informed, usually, than Uncle Babe. Asked didn't they trust anyone in the country, they said they felt the government should be the one—what's the government for. J. J.: Well, the people must see that the government. . . . The People: Well, they were busy getting in the hay. J. J.: If farmers can't get legislation who can, they're the mainstay. The Farmers: Our children learn that in school, lots of things, they learn wrong. Use the ballot? Yes, on election days they went to the polls and voted, yes, mainly against. In this country you have to be on your guard against the officers chosen. In the first place who chooses em? Oh yes, direct primary now. A certain governor had done sumpn for em, the prosperous ones first. Uncle John said this was a prosperous farming section, milk machines coming in for those who could afford them so join the co-op and sell your produce to us for more than you get elsewhere because we can ship it in large amounts at lower rates. He signed up some of them. Others he could believe could not pay to enter. He said to these latter that if he got enough signers he would pay their dues for them and he did that later. He could never bear misfortune and he wanted this venture to be a success. The other man who was to be associated with him was around in different nearby townships getting signers.

Uncle Babe returned home these nights, his sack of Red Lime Fertilizer gone. Matty understood he was paying his expenses each day by selling these. John hated to tell her otherwise. I had ridden along sometimes and it seemed to me he had left most of it here and there among the poorer farmers as a trial gift. Altogether, he was absorbed in his new work but he brooded over his pipe ways and means of moving on. Maybe what he really wanted was company, a close friendship, someone in prosperous circumstances perhaps—he worried over these other people. Many persons loved the poor and hard-working because it was to the interests of the former . . . he had to in the speeches he was going to make on Memorial Day and later on the subject of organization . . . he really wished they were different. To better these people, and through that make himself a place in the country, the state, the nation . . . if only he still had the old dog to talk to. Was seeing a great deal of Phoebe Hake, she, fifteen miles away.

Sometimes he would deliberately go out over the marsh that skirted the lake and woods, the shitepoke still as grass until John's voice rose up in behalf of the people. Determined now to prepare himself for the dynamics of platform work. No light matter for a man shy and starting to take on fat. He must have been haunted by dreams of speaking so well that cannons would greet him at the various towns and villages.

He called himself a Progressive, sure to mean militant liberal. Soon he was speaking in town halls and old opera houses. He memorized his speeches but if he forgot could always put in something else. His practice of throwing the voice at times like a hand grenade into the back seats made him a recognized orator of the day and out from the woods or gardens of the vaudeville curtains he stood against would come: The question is who shall rule, labor or the big producers who control through slavery the laborers? I tell you it is our duty to curb corporation power. We have inherited, as it were, the great idea that this country is the place for free competition and we mean to have it. I am coming, Ladies and Gentlemen, to the farmers' co-operative. (Quieter:) Such a farm movement was started a few years ago that for two years agriculture defeated the corporations. This can be done again. All we want is a fair profit. When we have established a farmers co-operative we will rest content. . . . After all, however much the economic conditions of the country stare us in the face we must look to the higher things of life . . . (Grenade:) You do want to possess this freedom from materialism. That boy of yours must have an education. . . . Uncle Babe maybe wished often that he could sink back into the sky of the curtain and be a pure idealist. And all the while the military bands. He may have remembered a former militant liberal in the state who had stuck to his post, had written way back in 1858 (in a letter to his wife but now the book is out). Uncle Babe would come away very hoarse from this kind of thing and very retiring. Sometimes on days of parades, unless he had to throw grenades into the ranks, he would join and march, the badges of his party and lodge upon him—never killed a man in his life, one old friend said. The liberal military air, a system of rank. Major F. and Commander St. B. were speakers even in peace.

John was still in the fish business in fall and spring. One of the working men was put in charge of the crew when John was away, and Matty was there. She let him go—his lime fertilizer must be going good, she thought. My mother helped with the cooking and Matty had a strong hand for business. When Matty called the men to dinner: Come now! she wasn't to be trifled with. Sometimes she'd jump into the gasoline launch, speed off down to the mouth of the river, circle around, watch the fishermen. She could handle a gun too, a good marksman. In many ways she was a better executive than her brother. As the men worked nearby she'd raise the window and call out how the rope should be passed or what kind of bolt or which parts should be put together next. John could always return to the executive mansion and find everything going at high pitch.

The old folks passed on. Great Uncle Gotlieb first. A stroke while in the woods, sat by a tree all night. His insurance company, Modern Woodman, failed. John had paid the assessments toward the last as they mounted, only to lose all. Made him dammad but of course, what could he do. The men in charge of the company were out of his reach. As time went on, thinking it over, he concluded perhaps the head men were business men used to taking profits and big salaries naturally; they couldn't understand that their salaries should be held down to the decent level of men giving service. An economist in England was way later to make that same excuse for the failure of a utility company in this country.

Riecky had stayed with my mother's mother in the north of the state as she grew older and not so well, and Grandma by way of Matty bought her gold belt buckle twice to help give the poor thing a feeling of security—she was always afraid she'd have to go to the Poor House. Wasn't long and she was gone too.

John was taking on more weight, becoming known, always advancing the cause of his leader and his party, and while he waited for things to take shape—give the people time, he said, they can't be hurried—he was opening up the land along the river into lots; could sell off a lot now and then, always a little income. The people out here did not catch an idea maybe as fast as city people. But when he thought of the masses in the city he was glad he was out here. Country people had more freedom. There in the city ground down by the industrial system—their minds were faster but could they show anything more for it?—came wandering out here sometimes either very much dressed up and no money to pay for drinks and a night's lodging, or looked very poor and spent their last nickel for drink and owed you besides— that element. He always spoke of the masses and the people as two different classes. Better to be out here, respectable owners of property, he said, better anyhow, do your own work, be your own boss. Beyond that, another class of big people who were everybody's—bosses?—he owned to the quaint separatist belief that some of these could have money control without oppressing others. In his day it was considered a good thing to liberate the mind but not to change it. Never too fast. Never appear eager for a livelihood. One had to have it but it wasn't nice to seem too eager, showed you were a gentleman of good taste not to seem hungry. J. J. had a way always of covering up money transactions, they were seldom direct. If he wanted to buy or sell something it worked through a third person who absorbed the taint, the profits. Usually lawyers, but also insurance and real estate men and even garage owners accustomed to out and out deals—they "had to take" houses, plows, furniture, in payment of debts. These masses of thirds—masses, Uncle John implied, had to work so hard and shamelessly—made business go round. Every decent family had its own or hired these ministers of buying and selling, hated and revered. They would line up prospective buyers for John's lots and hunting grounds, some of them John's own friends, and then he would choose the ones he thought would be interested and give a dinner for them, rather, Matty. But it turned out that those who really bought were the thirds on the staff of life seeing John was pinched at certain times and they could get a lot for a song. Matty had a greater respect for them than for the sportsmen who wouldn't spend so someone else could play too. She saw that the former got the best of everyone, were shrewd, saving, lived below their means and that's how they had something. It often brought her a spell of neuralgia and force as she saw how her brother must have a wild duck placed on each plate at his dinners and lose out. Later, by having eaten in the company of bankers he was to be able to borrow money. He said she must realize he was ahead there because not everyone during the depression could borrow money.

Cottages went up on the lots, they began to have neighbors.

Somebody was always wanting to use the ladder when Matty wanted it. The woods were not sold. Uncle John could come back from stumping the country for himself or this senator or that to the solitude of his woods, the trees overtopping him. Always in his simple honesty he gave the neighbors the run of his garage and when he'd be ready to start work around the place—his clothes all changed, overalls on—he'd go out and find his tools not there, jacks gone, ropes gone, hammers, axe. . . . But he considered he was helping someone so all well and good. He sighed. Never got ruffled. After all, he owed them something for buying the land. He went back into the house to be comfortable again. He didn't doubt the borrowers would return the things, he was honest. Matty thought if they didn't he'd still count em his friends because he'd have forgotten who borrowed what. And of course he had in mind they'd vote for him some day. He's too trusting, no wonder he can't do business, said Matty. I think myself he must have seemed to people to be so honest that he wasn't just nor keen. While they used him, knew they could depend on him, they looked with suspicion on a man who almost liquidated his property for the sake of his neighbors.

At last the day when the farmers came around, the co-op established, Uncle Babe in charge. He was winding up his fishing for good. Filling out his income tax blank the night the man brought the news that a meeting of those interested in the co-op would be held the next night to settle it. He had made out a tan blank, the wrong color, and was now on a green one. We were all sitting around, electric lights just installed. I was there, taking a few days off from business college (my father's insurance). Matty must have made her usual remark about income tax and the like: Cheez, if they'd offer a job instead of taking money away . . . well, it won't be long before they'll want yuh to keep track of the number of jobs yuh do and pay tax on em. As the man came in with the news, Josephine's daughter gave up her chair with a loud meow and doubtless caught her toes in the black and tan crocheted rugs as she jumped down and stretched. Beer and cigars were passed.

The next day Uncle Babe gave his tax blank to a lawyer acquaintance to fill out and drove off.

For three years he was to give the hammers and ladders of his honesty to the co-op and sit in comparative comfort in the office. Things started well. A merger was soon made with a national organization and for a period of five years J. J. served on county and state committees as well, white shirt every day and fine-dot tie, and so he was led up to the World War but he was just past draft age. Unable to speak now as much as he liked since he sincerely did not believe in the war, he nevertheless kept in touch through others with the general in Congress, the governor who had befriended him.

They won and rested. He saw though that he was still up against the same things: the always stronger "interests," the monopoly of power on the one side, and on the other the people of the agricultural community in a monopoly of sleep. He won an inch for the farmers, now the boom coming on—the only boom the farmers ever had was during the war—they relaxed. Things were going well even without the co-op. Their fight collectively slackened, as good as ended. Each farmer again competed with each. Wasn't it a free capitalist country? J. J. said they should continue the good work so as to prepare for times of shortage. Shortage? This was a prosperous farming section. Yes, but they must think what they would have for the next campaign. And they were doing better now, yet many of them, John noticed, refused tractors, telephones, vacation journeys. They mustn't slip into blind, unplanned production, he warned them. Price determines need!—all a matter of the people making it otherwise. He wrote in reply to my letters to him and Matty that the co-op leaders were holding picnics, giving out pop and ice cream cones free to induce people to come to their meetings. Some came, mainly children. It was like if you made an appointment they'd say: I'll see you yesterday. Never be different, J. J. told himself, so long as times stayed good. Of course he wished these times would stay. . . . Factory workers were faster, speedup, couldn't overeat. Out here the Middle Western Ages, farmers plodding behind their horses. Many drudged and denied themselves, put every penny in their farms, then sold or rented to retire to house and lot in town, their living going out of them—on the porch railing Will Farmer sat when he came to town, the basic principle of our government, the Will of the People. What could the people do against the money power now and always controlling the government? They must put men in power who could. J. J.'s chief, almost the only person who had dared militate against the war constantly called to the forces in his state to rally—freedom of the press, freedom of speech, tax the rich, curb the trusts—these things he was fighting for alone. J. J. would do the same. He would get himself endorsed by the leaders in the state. He would give a dinner, an influential standpat Republican would be invited along with the Progressives. To show they could be liberal minded. And La Follette had said, "Get and keep a dozen or more of the leading men in a community interested in, and well informed upon any public question and you have laid firmly the foundations of democratic government." They must plan so that good times would stay, or at least come oftener.

Uncle Babe retained his determination for public service through the years he was shunted from committee to committee, and then finally he was placed on the ticket. Quite well known by this time, men began coming to take even suppers with him. Matty had spells oftener.

To escape there were his acres and his radio. He liked to turn on the negro spirituals, the melting deep . . . Christ, how they could sing . . . the blackbirds settling down . . . he could forget about government. If he were asked about negroes he said they should be treated well but implied they shouldn't be given the upper hand. Matty had no time for radio. Was getting so all people wanted to do was sit and listen in. She didn't understand radio really—just foolish this guesswork pulled out of the air. She went on baking with luck, washing with an electric machine, sewing with the old tread—still made her summer dresses. Her broom in the kitchen would sweep on ceiling and sidewalls as well as floor in loud complaint of existing conditions, or she'd balance it against her, both arms going free.

One night a man and woman came out from the city, stayed over, in the morning bought the old place—the hotel and five acres surrounding. John liked this sudden, almost accidental business deal, made him happy and Matty was glad he needn't entertain the state about it. They had, for a few years past, given up using the hotel as a hotel, and now the cottage they'd planned immediately took shape on the other side of the grove, facing the river still, same view of woods and river from the windows, besides a new vegetable garden, flower garden, new arbors, chicken coop, pier. And next to their own cottage John built one to rent out—soon it would be his and Phoebe's. Very little woodland was sold with the old place, couldn't take the risk, might disappear overnight—John took only the dead wood for his fuel, and the mass of the woods standing there was protection on the north and something to look at. Would have to be pinched hard to sell any more trees.

Soon settled down again. Some of the old furniture was brought over. Their five rooms were large enough, many windows, and John's room—he allowed no curtains there, only shades. He had a little walnut cupboard for tobacco, a cot, a desk, small heater, radio. Most winter evenings they sat together in the kitchen, played euchre, dropped their apple peelings into the coal scuttle, Matty's short, quick-cut, John's round and round, unbroken.

Though less to do here, Matty was still in her neuralgic and head troubles, a woman demanding help, so used to men working on the place that during housecleaning days when she wanted stove or ice box moved she'd say, They can do this anytime now, I'm ready. Thereby she took in the neighbors. Private property before life. And as time went on she knew the courts upheld her. When the strikes came on in Detroit she read: "The right of an owner to his property is upheld by the circuit court." But the problem of neighbors staying to sit or to use the now fewer and fewer Beefelbein tools she could not always control as she liked. She was always ahead though. Her little business with her hens was fair. In one way or another she had managed to save $1000. Even during the depression she continued to gamble on her stock market, to pocket little revenues and clip coupons on coffee and soap.

The monopoly of sleep expanding. But Uncle John was running for the Assembly. He may have dreamed of serving the nation in the coming Presidential campaigns, of being called to conventions here or there: We need your help to nominate Hyle. Or Payne. Or Beefelbein. But the crash came, and then the depression, without him.

And April elections followed, sun and rain, Prairie Chickens, Phoebe . . . was still working in a drug store, giving a little each week to her mother, had asked John to invest her savings—turned out bad—made a feeling between them that should never have arisen, but he was now confident of getting into office and providing for them all.

Party feeling was intense while men huddled under a bridge and streets of people slowly died of hunger.

J. J. had been endorsed by party leaders and they were cheered when they spoke. At last a real start. Several important issues, but they had to limit themselves to what one address could adequately hold. For J. J. that meant principally the question of putting people back to work and a system of relief. On this he could give his whole heart, sound radical even, socialistic, though of course he was really becoming a Progressive Democrat soon voting for the Franklin D. Roosevelt deal.

Three days before spring election when the voters would declare themselves—for him—J. J. went out to the haystack to practice his speech of thanks to the people for supporting him. Trying out a new tone-placement to be ready for outdoor engagements. Matty, stepping out the back door heard: two million five hundred thousand. And again something like: three billion seven hundred twenty-six million. . . . The former likely the number of unemployed or the number of times he'd thought of them. Matty seeing the garden unplowed, a boat unrepaired, probably a fence down: no ground work, only figgers, figgers.

Election time, she thought, just mouth to mouth. People were living that way now instead of better. The newly married couple renting the cottage—They've got nothing, she said, go without hats or caps in winter, they live from mouth to mouth.

But to go back to Uncle Babe in the haystack, sheltered from the ill wind of depression . . . when it did strike him, poor man, he was not influential enough to keep out of the newspapers. In fact that very noon a man drove into the yard telling him the utility company which had both their savings was down so low that he feared it would never come back, and the next day it got around. Now the people still had, many of them, the feeling that a man to lose $8000, 8000 eggs in one basket, must be a poor business man . . . the system that permitted investment and crash was bad, of course, but every man must take care of himself. And doubtless, regarding John, the amount of his failure grew as it spread . . . $18,000 . . . $28,000 . . . someone said, I heard $38,000. So it passed from mouth to mouth and burned them up. Enemy papers, the day before election made the most of it. The organs of the opposition attacked me most bitterly, but I am in fighting trim and I feel confident of victory ahead . . . so an older, richer, nationally known mosquito-in-the-brush had long ago said favorably to the millions, a lawyer he became for the property holders of Milwaukee—Since lawyers, he'd said, in times of depression like the present are the only class that prospers. Uncle John couldn't fight now. Whether he just hadn't built up a successful campaign for himself, or the people were suspicious and resentful of a man in their midst who'd had enough money to retire before he was old . . . at any rate, he lost out.

He saw himself now suffering with the rest. His life past the middle, soon gone . . . what was it for? No use trying to sell any land now, nobody could buy. Mortgage the house, the woods, no, keep away from pain . . . go back to the Indians, they were happy . . . until their lands were taken away.

Night. Went to his room, the window. The big dipper, couldn't see it, different now . . . why did it move around, different positions? What were the stars? Maybe we weren't meant to know. If he'd broken into education a little further? They probably taught some damthing to fool the people. We learn wrong.

Next morning Matty baked without luck. Well, they still had cheese and their home.

He went over the land, heard bullfrogs—he'd had them imported a few years before, saw the yellow-heads in the rushes, the little river and the lake, all in a land of slavery, blue heron stands, finish, form, if city folks could see, advanced into summer, took his new stand against the bankers. Government control of . . . same radio cushion . . . money, credit. Setback, had a cold since April . . . government now controlled by it, wrong, but give it time. Change money. The government wouldn't have to be changed, would it?—not overthrown by . . . coughing. He felt as unsteady as a Whittier voter, or he began to feel what was best but couldn't bring himself to it. What was this talk of classes, anyway. But yes, if only the middle class and lower class would join together. Feed a cold, starve a fever. As a liberal, Uncle John did both, and the interests of both classes lost their point simultaneously. He was afraid that something must be done, anything though to keep a nation from passing away.

Think of it, I told Uncle Babe, goes down in the ocean, this country, bubbles, is gone! Not a plant to grow a whisker on. J. J. jumping in after it with a book on Money: What It Is. There it is!—the masses of workers with a government which is themselves and by them the mines, factories, forests, farms, railroads, banks, owned, and the right to work guaranteed, vacation too! A reasonable profit? No, all profit went down in the ocean, so did graft. Down with a fierce love of independence, Hamilton! Look, "our" woods. In your old age a pension and your same old pride a new one. A living science working for just such good Russ . . . Germans as you. Organized methods. Powerful tractors. Price-decline. Production costs in the barn fell and the haystack moved to the consumer!

The food which Matty always allowed John to provide was not very nourishing now, she said, only common, coarse food. He brought home less meat, almost no candy. Apples, lemons, were high. If only somebody would give a dinner, show they remembered what he'd done for them and give him a job. To help others. He'd worked hard in his younger days and since, to keep what he had. Now he'd have been ready to give his time and money for other concerns.

Farmers, organize for the benefit of society. But collective farming? Not own their land? Could a man be depended on to work land he didn't own? What people want is better living, walnut furniture, pottery, violets, theatres. . . .

Maybe some man put in control. Hard to know which one to trust. In 1912 the American people had elected President Wilson on the belief that he would lower the cost of living! Sometimes it was Wilson, sometimes the Pope, then again Coughlin, or the local police officer.

He met a man one day. We were riding home in John's Ford V8. I was on vacation—had taken a cut, working now for $2 a week more than room and board. The elderberry bushes beside the road were holding out their white blossom-plates where the pies would come. This man walking, dusty, a small sackload on his back, held out his hand.

J. J.: Going far?

Man: West, I guess, wherever I can find work. Know of any?

He had worked 35 years, it turned out, and now had nothing. John gave him some of our rolls and bananas and 50¢.

Uncle John worried over him. Pressure to bear. Yes, but as a whole, he said, the common people didn't know what was good for them, couldn't govern themselves. My uncommon Uncle! I suppose he couldn't forget they had repudiated him at the polls, but he said the more prosperous farmers were against relief for those in the towns who had nothing and if they didn't watch out they wouldn't have a friend in the legislature. They really didn't appreciate what was done, could be done, for them—he was led to this belief once long ago when he had given a ditch, a right-of-way straightout to a group of men who wanted to buy it. They never even thanked him. I saw his sadness, couldn't tell him just then that people don't want things done for them. He went on that he at least had a place to be in these hard times. Still, that man, and there must be many more, would see the ocean . . . if he had good luck, whereas he, John Beefelbein, had no means of seeing it, had to stay on in his old place.

He would gladly give the man more sackloads if he could.

o

Stage Directions

The window woman whose dress has been hung and draped looks out. There's a wax-wing on every leaf, hay background, state-craft, salve smell and lavish retort. Shh . . . the man with the juniper growth to his beard,—bankers leave their wives to their safes and redouble openings. They walk around the oblong and Oh·is the heart of the modern furniture. Once out the knock is on the other side. I seem to take *un ciel*, a circle in another tongue. Have we experienced a cycle from which we are likely to recover, or have we seen the death of an era? A loop of blue light shows white organdie ruffles herself. My hat—it was taken for a flight—too sad for my face to assume. Young escort bows. I can't pick a thing up and bring it to successive stages. Yet for what we see the mind has to sink down out of sight—perhaps not possible for us. But think how paultry: the common black and white, the break-fast table and then all the rest of the meals. We have our limberger but we mustn't bring it to the table. Have you been married? Yes, I've been attacked. The ring of light flames as on comes the night scene from Tremulus Asps. Somebody sleeps under the oatshed and resets his pudding. Tieci Tape-over's buttons shine. He points. I wish there was something to listen to particularly. Wuzz or whir. His wife says he used to work in a factory; now he's a gentleman—runs a beer tavern. But he doesn't exercise enough. If only he could make himself tired. Blackness soughs as a matter of light-ing. Fanatic acid. Constructions gleam—triangles and verbal arra. Inimical Pop-its down front kneeling in swift, strange prayers as-sure the world they're dangerous. See how it brings the red swing closer.

o

The History of Old Abe the War Eagle
(Bald Eagle)

8th Wisconsin Infantry

Old Abe, the Wisconsin War Eagle, was captured in his boyhood in the wilds of the Flambeau river in the spring of 1861, from a nest in a tall pine tree about seven miles up the river from Park Falls. Taken from nest by an Indian, known in later life as Chief Charley of the Lac du Flambeau band of Chippewa Indians. Some called him Chief Sky. The Indians brought him down the Flambeau river that spring into Chippewa. Chief Sky was the son of Thunder of Bees, Chief of the Flambeau band of Chippewas, and he sold the eagle to Mrs. D. McCann of Jim Falls for a bushel of corn, whose husband sold the eagle to John Jeffries of Eau Claire. Mr. Jeffries then presented the eagle to Captain John E. Perkins of the Eau Claire Badgers, Company C of the 8th Regiment. The eagle was then sworn into the U.S. service as Old Abe, the mascot and decorated with red, white, and blue ribbons and a rosette of the same colors. A standard was made on which he could be carried. Captain Perkins was offered $200 for the eagle but Capt. said, "The eagle belongs to the company, and no money can buy him."

In Madison at Camp Randall, an immense crowd of people gathered and as the regiment marched into camp, the eagle expanded his wings, and seized a corner of the American flag that was floating over him, and carried it in his beak all through the march. In St. Louis, Capt. Perkins was offered $500 for the eagle but Capt. said, "I would just as soon sell one of my men."

At the battle of Corinth, the Confederate General Price ordered his men to be sure and capture him if they could. If they could not capture him, to kill him, adding he would rather get that bird than the whole regiment.

During a battle, his appearance was perfectly magnificent. At the sound of the regimental bugle, which he had learned to recognize, he would start suddenly, dart up his head, and then bend it gracefully, anticipating the shock. When the battle commenced, he would spring up and spread his wings, uttering his startling scream, heard, and felt, and gloried in by all the soldiers. The fiercer and louder the storm, the fiercer, louder, and wilder were his screams.

During the engagements he suffered but few slight wounds, and returned home to Madison hale and hearty. In 1880, at the soldiers' reunion at Milwaukee, Old Abe was carried in the procession. He was sleek and majestic, a complacent creature of the forest. General Grant and Old Abe were the honored guests of this military reunion. When the band played he uttered his battle scream, consisting of five or six wild trilling notes in quick succession. In the winter of 1881 a fire started in the Wisconsin State Capitol where Old Abe spent his days. On Mar. 26, 1881, with a slight tremor Old Abe expired in the arms of his keeper, George Gillis.

The 8th Wis. regiment took part in 32 battles.

An eagle was found (belonged to American Legion post at (Mellon, Wis.) and presented to the state in 1933, taking the place of the Old Abe. This eagle is now mounted and placed in the center of the large hall of the GAR rooms.

o

Untitled

The evening's automobiles, men from work, shot silently through green lights. Encased motors give man the swift, shining precision that his mind as he drives can't give him. Well, he makes his get-away in beauty. He passes gleaming. And somewhere along the speedway for men with motors is home, woman.

I must have been aglow myself as I stood there—I was a banner headline in running lights: YOUNG MAN GOES HOME—after twenty years as newspaper printer. Although mid-twentieth century of the middle ages continued had brought me the printing press, I'd found that Wm. James was right: "The sensational press is the organ of a state of mind which means a new 'dark' ages that may last more centuries than the first one. Then illiteracy was brutal and dumb and power was rapacious without disguise. Now illiteracy has an enormous literary organization and power is sophistical;" and this organization, as good an avenue for plunder as any business is, protects and is protected by that other and still more expensive organization, war. I'd found that a job does not necessarily sustain life. Grime, guts, gloom, the crash and roar of the big presses, speed, overtime speed, reason jarred. Throw the forms away for the last time, I was away to my childhood home in the country.

Benj glided up to the curb in his own silent, white tired speed-gleam. I recalled my sister's remark on a certain small red beauty in the neighborhood, "They've bought a hummingbird—you can't haul anything with it."

"But why do you do it," shrieked Benj, "It's lunacy!—alone, isolated, when everybody else is gearing himself for the fight for survival."

"Are men afraid of their own selves? Give us peace and we'll survive."

"But nobody to talk with!"

"Talk, these days, is dangerous. My friend the poet says 'Talk is a form of love'. Maybe I'll find that form in the millenium after the next."

"And what about Norma? Aren't you marrying her in June?"

"Why is it that women about to be married need a mineralogical fulfilment—silver, diamond?"

"You'll find a flood. In that lowland in the spring it won't take a forked stick to find water. What *do* you expect to find?"

"The ancient present. In me the years are flowing together."

I awoke the next morning to twitterings out of leaves on every side, mixed with a marsh hush that I must have known soon after I'd known life in this world. The river had risen in the back land to within six feet of the house. Here in the lush wash, you go back to the exuberant source and start over. My mother, not too happily married, lived on her nerves on this stream, hunted and fished, grew flowers as big as plates in the Nile-like silt and said—how often she said it—"I've got a new pain."

The goddam dragon flies mating all over hell, said Jackie from my office, once long ago, and Jackie was a lady, unintellectual but enlightened, one to whom diamonds held no lure.

No lady is the other office woman by her own insistence, weak-voiced and slight of build though she is. She is the proof reader, Francie Canoye who sits in her monastic, windowless cell, abhorrent of anything approaching profanity, but who manages to domineer over some sixteen men—printers, editors, bosses—with a desperate, old maid, bitter, obscene purity.

Francie's impeccably penciled initials in the corner of her galleys soon stood among us men for Finance Capitalism. This small piece of steel flesh with a bad heart and spleen, a military bearing which was her only patrimony, maintains a deadly hatred of labor unions despite a ready acceptance of holiday pay. Two weeks paid vacation she never gets because she refuses it on the grounds that there is no one to whom she can trust her job.

This is the woman who carries her portable possessions to and from work with her every day in a big bag resembling an enormous, pendulous, inverted bladder, never trusting their safety with her landlady. Sometimes the bag contains empty milk bottles—her own serious admission—to protect herself against landlady and landlord should the situation arise. Actually, she has nothing. A brother who died of leukemia had thereby depleted his and her own savings. Poor old thing, she marches along the street under the heavy weight of nothing. If she'd had money, she'd have quit—no, more likely as the self-appointed carrier of civilization she'd have gone on suffocating at her post. It's generally agreed that Francie knows her gothics and her futuras, but day after day of stepped-up tensions, dead lines, the whole deadly, competitive madness, have left their mark. And natural that sheer noise should affect her as she grows older. Not that she would complain to the owners. She looked belligerent, one particularly distressing day, when even her young copyholder shouted in near delirium, "Can't hear the stars, too close to the big press."

Through an age of violence and sudden death such as ours, a culture that hardly distinguishes between credulity and superstition, a culture that forever oscillates between a search for a movie with a Holy Grail theme and a search for the next meal, proof reader Francie Canoye guides her once sharp mind by sheer force of will.

"Triskaidekaphobia thought they'd stump me on that one they didn't get me on Capuchin and bailiwick either Christ was a Jew they say—impossible! take it back to the editors I'm afraid of Frank Dane's bull neck the linotype boys are late today and sloppy we need a Hitler over here to make things move the moon changes tomorrow so we'll get different weather do you pray?" And when Francie runs on thus the ads in the night's paper loom up with tender *lions* for tender *loins*, or *grease-free* ginghams for *crease-free* ginghams or unconditional *surrender* (on tires) instead of unconditional *guarantee*. So she loses her night's sleep and starts the morning of the next day by laying into the men who had failed to make the corrections which if marked hadn't been changed because the proofs had come back too late from the proof reader's desk. At such a time her grey figure stood before you like the sandpiper's out at my yard's "shore line", a clam shell on long, thin legs with nervous-nodding head. Once a child came along, asked what kind of a bird that was and "What does it kill?" The truth was that often in her "brute goodness", her only laxative from tight-bound days and too many candy bars, was to let an error fly where it would among the stench along her own close-confined portion of beach.

But now I—at least I—was home. I looked toward the water's edge where lay milk bottle, electric light bulb, whiskey flask. China's great blue heron, Poor Joe, look at him go. A knock at the door—who in hell? I hung from a cold cigarette. A woman, her hair burning in the morning sun.

"Parachute?"

"No, I'm one of the last of my line—legs." She stood there with more than one range of intensity and a basket of chicken and salad. It was Marion Dollman from the hill.

"Come in." We sat at table. Five feet from us on the other side of the window a yellow warbler was busy at her compact nest, three eggs of her own and a cowbird's. The birds building in the bush under my nose!

The girl passed the salt. "You look at me as though you expected to find something of a world . . ." The world, we said, will come from scientists on the tail of their terror-literature, if it comes. Still, we'd make our own.

"Tell me", she said, "What do you know to be true? Not merely that roughly radiation dies away according to the formula r equals one over time."

"Not roughly. Knowing goes best with the quietest touch. Otherwise it's somebody else's stuff. Even so I can only indicate."

Her tender-spoken "No terror here." And "With all deference to what we could be together, no two persons can ever become one, each must be free to desire what the other has indicated. At least we'd make it a point, wouldn't we, never to be familiar no matter how close we got?"

"And together, isolated from a great portion of humanity, as all with feeling are, these days . . . while the flood recedes and the grass starts fast to mow me in my prime."

"Isn't it glorious? Let's trim green thought in one place and let it grow wild in another."

The lovely greenery—I hadn't too much of it in my pocket or in any bank. But we don't need a third of the things, the sheer, literal litter that people do in our savage cities.

Let's sit here in the long afternoon and last.

Notes:
all about the virgin is out! Too pretentious—you saw that.

No title as yet—your "The evening's Automobiles"—well, something like that along line of *moving*, something that has to do with mind moving so as to unite all time etc. . . or: 'Brute Goodness' or Renaissance . . .

I feel queer too as a man! I could print it under a man's name! No.

1. "Why should we honour those that die upon the field of battle a man may show as reckless a courage in entering into the abyss of himself." (This is Yeats, but I won't credit him, I guess?)

2. It was abrupt you said with just saying "and said"—I don't feel that's so—it wouldn't be in poetry necessarily. But maybe you like this better.

3. Some things in life are not credible as fiction! She actually did carry milk bottles and for that purpose, she said. A great many things about her I can't tell—just wouldn't be believed.

4. I've used spaces to give the eye the confusion in her mind.

5. Here's my "brute goodness", won't use it if I use it as title.

6. This maybe I'd better omit— she was socially unacceptable, taking a laxative and then f ting all afternoon. Or it could be interpreted differently and melt in with the rest of that paragraph's horror.

Nevermind spelling—my dictionary says dead line, two words— always look of everything before I send 'em out. ( )

Thanks—I know you're busy

o

SWITCHBOARD GIRL

I divined this comedy, Dante, before I went in. But I had to have a job. "Like one who has imperfect vision, we see the things which are remote from us." O brother, we saw tho the eyes were shot. We had light if not love. We had business.

Nystagmus ("The poet's eye, in a fine frenzy rolling"), the searching movement, combined with 80% vision. You'll have to use a magnifying glass, we can't give you glasses to reach print. Good-bye to proof reading. Good-bye to a living. No! That low, rangy, glass-walled office and plant in the Frank Lloyd Wright setting, clean-mowed acres, tulips, petunias, evergreens—I would apply there. Not literature but light fixtures and pressure cookers. Out of daylight into Wade Light.

I was the September dandelion—forty, female—seeking a place among the young fluorescent petunias. I keep cropping up in the world's backyards while here in America, on all sides they shear civilization back to the seventeen-year-old girl, not yet young shall we say.

I entered the window-walled office of personnel. Or was it a corner of a little theatre? What would the director be like? A properly placed man may expand his influence over the whole of your sight. We met ideally, as strangers do, without prejudice, without violence . . . courteous before the guessed-at depth. All art between us. Will he help me? He is not usual. He moves as in a dance to be considerate. As if to speak, against the room's outdoor backdrop, of Renoir? Of Einstein? Is he the master economist with a sense of the relative value of things? The artist with a sense of needing fewer things? The political observer with a knowledge of electronics? What does he know really, sweetly, by touch?

He said, "You read."

Beethoven: "It is impossible to say to people, 'I am deaf'." But I said it: I have an eye handicap.

"I wonder if you should . . . we have a switchboard opening. You might try it."

I went in. Lights, polished glass, blond satin finished desks, glossy haired and bald-headed efficiency. Shine. Lamps to be produced. Lamps to be sold. The antique sweatshop base with a new shine. You'll never have to polish this brass, a lacquering process, won't tarnish. This is the lust that will never rust.

The shade by the door, the grey parchment face, cracked in a half smile. Shall I appear alive or let myself be carried along? I suppose man is, the most sensitive physical part of him, an electrical apparatus, switches, wires, etc. . . . . How much do I give to Wade lamps? It takes 1028 human bodies to build a star. Purely business.

The girl at the switchboard shouted, "Come in—if you can—it's my birthday, you know. Once a year and at Christmas this happens—nylons, table lamps, candy, help yourself. The bosses, the old honeypots, must like me a little bit, anyhow. Sit down. Let me tell you what goes. They're all good enough guys, family men, church, golf, they're after the business, they'll lay on you, of course."

You see in a place of this kind, she said, the switchboard girl is one of their outlets. They do a great deal of their sweating thru you. You'll make the contact and in haste, also they relax thru you. You're a part of it when their bags are full and you jazz 'em when they're down.

"Get me the Howard Hotel, a single."

"Good, I like to sleep close."

That was Mendau, the burnt-out fuse in the beautiful suit who still thinks he's got something to sell.

"Give me Philadelphia." Give me Europe. I'm waiting, operator, for the Paris pick-up. I'm on wartime Montparnasse, gas mask, phosphorescent heels, illuminated brooch. "What's that?" What does it look like? There they call it what it is.

The Japs: We had neither hens nor eggs. We went requisitioning. A miserable village. On the way back we began to look for Chinese girls.

They don't make 'em as sensitive as geiger counters.

"Goddamit what the hell happened to that call to Lethal Steel? Sleeping at the switchboard?"

"I reported to you, sir, that Dan Blaine will talk."

"Christ if you can't get anybody but Dead-End Daniel—"

"What was the name they wanted?" Somebody by the name of Christ.

Please pass the blood. Human matériel is obsolescing.

As for the work itself, she plays an intricate chess. You gamble with the red and the white and the green, without benefit of spa.

I lost. "No natural aptitude."

Dante? Yes, go ahead.

END

Three Reviews

A Test of Poetry. Louis Zukofsky. Brooklyn, NY: The
Objectivist Press, 165pp. $3.00.

Zukofsky's arrangement is as clean in form as its criticism and
the good example of poetry it offers. It is appraised correctly on
the jacket of the book by Clifton Fadiman, Mark Van Doren and
William Carlos Williams. Distilled excellence, rich portions from
the poets from Homer thru the present, some of these difficult—
poetry is not soft—supported by Zukofsky's precise interpretive
remarks. "The lines of poetry of great emotional significance in
any age are rare. To obtain, therefore, an accurate criticism of
them and of the lesser work which surrounds them, reading
should not shun analysis." To read for pleasure, this is the aim
here. Poetry out of the "living processes" of everyday and from
there "to always another phase of existence"—the worlds needs it.

What makes certain lines of poetry good and others not so
good? Part II, the pivot for the entire book, begins so far as Zu-
kofsky's remarks are concerned: "A simple order of speech is an
asset in poetry." Next, in the section, regarding William Morris'
roundabout translation of Homer: "He is piling it on thin." And
we're off. Parts I and III offer more examples of good poetry, but
without comment or authors' signatures—to add to the zest of a
lovely game. A turn to the chronological chart shows the full use
of an index with titles, authors, dates when supplemented by stan-
dards such as "content," "emotion," "inevitability," "measure." A
book for the general sensitive reader—in classroom and out.

Zukofsky is moved, of course, by certain perceptions: the ex-
act word; any word a poetic word "if used in the right order, with
the right cadence, with a definite aim in view"; song, "one of the
mainsprings of poetry"; a poem: "an emotional object" close to
the people and their experiences, i.e., the source, something to
put your hands on as against metaphysical rockers; "in any age"
. . ."The lasting attraction in the words of a poem and its con-
struction make it classic and contemporary at the same time."

In this day of adding machines in bookstores' windows, of
comic greeting cards (Hello Grandma with the unstretchable cor-
set), the surface tilt, the armed avoidance of quiet, of deep satis-
faction, a book is printed. In this day when girls catching a boy
with a book ask, "who's the young Einstein," *A Test of Poetry* sur-
veys this as well as poetry, charged and in its place. The book
could be bigger—the reader can make it so. Omissions—at first
glance—until one realizes that it is more than an anthology.

o

> To record and elate for all time . . . (poems)
> based on nothing less than the world, the entire
> humanly known world.
>
>   o

> Good verse is determined by the poet's suscepti-
> bilities involving a precise awareness of differ-
> ences, forms and possibilities of existence—
> words with their own attractions included. The
> poet, no less than the scientist, works on the as-
> sumption that inert and live things and relations
> hold enough interest to keep him alive as part of
> nature.
>
>   o

> Felt deeply, poems like all things have the possi-
> bilities of elements whose isotopes are yet to be
> found. Light has travelled and so looked forward.
>   Poetry—For My Son When He Can Read

Twenty-five years before he wrote these statements in behalf
of poetry, Zukofsky began his long poem "*A*." It was strange at
that moment of time and at that point in space. Many writers and
readers, unless travelling at the same speed, have lost contact with
"*A*" and some who wore dark glasses then are now beginning
to see.

It is understandable that Lawrence Durrell, living in countries
other than the United States and so probably unaware of "*A*,"
should be thinking now along the same lines: "Time has become
. . . welded in space—no longer the quickly flowing river of the
Christian hymns moving from here to there along a marked series
of stages. But an always present yet always recurring thing." "*A*"
presents an order of succession but also of interweaving themes
uniting with new and related matter, tightening often into such
forms as canzones or ballades the tonality of our speech. The poet
asked himself early in the poem: "*Can/ The design/ Of the fugue/
Be transferred/ To poetry?*"

Technically, a recurring thing, for all but the apathetic stu-
dent, is never the same—though the *idea* of *recurrence* is useful to
establish relationships, to reveal kinship. There were journeys

---

through past hells, heavens—flowing rivers still navigable by degrees. Zukofsky's hell is today's and the good he finds is today's. From the incident of a performance of Bach's *St. Matthew Passion* at Carnegie Hall the poem moves to make the singing, living machine of our time. Now with some 200 pages of "*A*"—twelve movements—we see that here is one who has always been coming to where he is and who wants to know what he has to live through to get further. Whether he writes of love or inanimate objects or cities or minds, our usual notion of poem is bound to be upset a little by the constant electronic interaction. "Three or four things occur at a time making the difference between Aristotelian expansive unities and the concentrated locus which is the mind acting creatively upon the facts."—Z. in his preface to *An Objectivists Anthology*.

"'How journeyed?'/ Journeyed./ With an impulse to master/ music and related matters." ("*A*"—8)

> My one voice. My other: is
> An objective—rays of the object brought to a
>   focus,
> An objective—nature as creator—desire
>   for what is objectively perfect
> Inextricably the direction of historic and
>   contemporary particulars. ("*A*"—6)

As for Spinoza: "He who creates/ Is a mode of these inertial systems—/ The flower—leaf around leaf wrapped around the center leaf" ("*A*"—6)

Journeyed. Overheard on a side street after the performance of the *Passion*:
"The Pennsylvania miners . . . the thing's/ becoming a mass movement." ("*A*"—1)

To Reno—"Divorced from himself." ("*A*"—6)

Saluting friends and other poets, and Bach's *Passion*:

> "There are different techniques,
> Men write to be read, or spoken,
> Or declaimed, or rhapsodized,
> And quite differently to be sung";
> "I heard him agonizing,
> I saw him *inside*";
> "Everything which
> We really are and never quite live."

Far into (about three) in the morning,
The trainmen wide awake, calling
Station on station, under earth, ("*A*"—1)

Boy and girl—"Breath fast as in love's lying close,/ Crouched
high—O my God, into the flower!" ("*A*"—2) And "On that Sun-
day, in the wind, in the night,/ in the grasses,/ Were prostrated a
thousand asses—/ Lads' and lasses'" ("*A*"—6) . . ."Our aged
heads are our homes/ We had a Speech, our children have/ evolved
a jargon./ Even the Death has gone out of us—we are void."
("*A*"—4)

But I tell you this man had vistas:—
Ties, handkerchiefs to match,
Mufflers, dress shirts, golf holes,
Chocolate eclaires, automobiles and entrées.
  ("*A*"—6)

And of horses: "In another world/ We will not motor."
("*A*"—3) We may not, say the wooden sawhorses of "*A*"—7, the
kicking horse rhythm and the flying manes of words—horseplay
if it were not so serious. The poet resolves his criticism of poetry
into the movement of the poem. "Street closed." The seven dig-
gers work on a street with eyes closed, ears closed. "From me to
them no singing gut" since everything says, including the poet
"We want a meal, different techniques." Names and ideas from
previous movements of "*A*" are brought in again: Ricky, livefor-
ever, Shimaunu-San, clavicembalo. The theme of "*A*"—7 is one
that not everyone writing knows, even yet, this far past the
depression: that an intellectual, an artist, must sit on a stoop by
himself when everybody else has "strayed," if they were there, "on
a manhole."

And now we come to the eight themes of "*A*"—8, at least
eight: 1, Labor as creator, as creature; 2, burial of Jesus in connec-
tion with the *Passion* and what is to be said now; 3, Bach's life in
relation to all this and the previous parts of "*A*" and what it means
to the poet, how others might look at it, friends, different men-
talities, continuation of "different techniques" theme, Kay etc. in
earlier movements; theme 4, a history of history, composition as
action; theme 5, a chapter of American and international history;
6, of the nature of things; 7, matter thinking, bodily substance;
reflections of themes 5, 6, 7 in contemporary science: physics,
mathematics ("Infinite is a meaningless word: except—it states/

That our mind is capable of performing/ an endless process of addition.") Each theme pumped with the sound of an organ modulates into or is heard against the other, until all go together. In music you would have eight voices, here the words suggest all eight at once as the poem grows. A lecturer on modern art recently said it can't just say this is a bad century, if it does,—it must show how it holds together. Zukofsky, in presenting economics and politics, is, for all that, interested in recording a poem, in holding together the parts: "And of labor:/ Light lights in air,/ on streets, on earth, in earth—/ Obvious as that horses eat oats—/ Labor as creator,/ Labor as creature,/ To right praise." And without predatory intent:

> By the green waters oil
> The air circles the wild flower; the men
> Skirt along the skyscraper street and carry
>   weights
> Heavier than themselves;
> By the rotted piers where sunk slime feeds
>   the lily-pads,

> Not earth's end.
> The machines shattering invisibles
> And which wrecked the still life
> Precede the singling out; the setting up of things
> Uphold the wrist's force; and
> The blood in the ear
> Direction of the vertical
>   rigidly bound to the head, the
>   accelerated motion
>   of rotation of the head
> Under the head's hair.
> SOCONY will not always sign off on this air.

"Dear Friend, when/ I die, but/ I'm not dead./ Song?/ After
        bread."

> *Isenacum en musica,* hear us
> Digging—we are singing of gardens—March
> Day of equal night, Bach's *chorus primus*
> To *chorus secundus* to the groined arch—
> To vanish as the cone fruit of the larch:
> Voice a voice blown, returning as May, dew

On night grass: and he said I worked hard, hue
Of word on the melody, (each note worth
Thought the clatter of a water-mill drew):
Labor, light lights in air, on earth, in earth.

  The First Half of "A"—9, published in 1940, works economic
value and some concepts of modern physics into the canzone
form. Here again, Zukofsky is concerned with making a poem.
"*A*"'s ethics and politics are as old as Aristotle from whom Marx
took, or as old as Xenophanes (who took from the Old Testa-
ment?) or The Book of the Dead: a distinction between use and
unnatural use. The prose statement on the form tells us of the
mathematical analogue used in translating the music of Cavalcan-
ti's *Donna Mi Prega* into English. "The ratio of the accelerations of
two sounds (r,n) has been made equal to the ratio of the accelera-
tions of the coordinates (x,y) of a particle moving in a circular
path with uniform angular velocity." As a poet's labor of today the
difficulties of transliterating internal and end rhyme, odd asso-
nance and consonance, eleven syllables and four main stresses to a
line, all of another century, were not enough. "Applied mathe-
matics employs a quantity called 'Action' defined as the product of
energy and time. Perhaps things are such quanta of 'Action' when
they are defined as time congealed labor." Zukofsky turned labor
as abstraction "into the labor present in the words of the song
itself" (*Restatement*, "*A*"—9). The second half of "*A*"—9 is an-
other canzone, the rhyme almost identical with that of the first—
the 13th century prosody and love—recapitulated in its 20th cen-
tury definition as calculus of thought, but thought that still has a
shape: and so it balances the economics and physics of the first
half. Readers will not notice the calculus, only the sound, the en-
ergy, and that is the art of it. A great deal of modern art and
literature is tissue wrapping paper, not stuff that is tough. Zukof-
sky's stuff is tough. The first two strophes and coda of the first
half are:

        An impulse to action sings of a semblance
        Of things related as equated values,
        The measure all use is time congealed labor
        In which abstraction things keep no resemblance
        To goods created; integrated all hues
        Hide their natural use to one or one's neighbor.
        So that were the things words they could say:
          Light is

Like night is like us when we meet our mentors
Use hardly enters into their exchanges,
Bought to be sold things, our value arranges;
We flee people who made us as a right is
Whose sight is quick to choose us as frequenters,
But see our centers do not show the changes
Of human labor our value estranges.

Values in series taking on as real
We affect ready gold a steady token
Flows in unbroken circuit and induces
Our being, wearies of us as ideal
Equals that heady crises eddy. Broken
Mentors, unspoken wealth labor produces,
Now loom as causes disposing our loci,
The foci of production: things reflected
As wills subjected; formed in the division
Of labor, labor takes on our imprecision—
Bought, induced by gold at no gain, the close
    eye
And gross sigh fixed upon gain have effected
Value erected on labor, prevision
Of surplus value, disparate decision.
  o

We are things, say, like a quantum of action
Defined product of energy and time, now
In these words which rhyme now how song's
    exaction
Forces abstraction to turn from equated
Values to labor we have approximated.

Of the second half:

An eye to action sees love bear the semblance
Of things, related is equated,—values
The measure all use who conceive love, labor
Men see, abstraction they feel, the resemblance
(Part, self-created, integrated) all hues
Show to natural use, like Benedict's neighbor
Crying his hall's flown into the bird: Light is
The night isolated by stars (poled mentors)

Blossom eyelet enters pealing with such changes
As sweet alyssum, that not-madness, (ranges
In itself, there tho acting without right) is—
Whose sight is rays, "I shall go; the frequenters
That search our centers, love; Elysium
     exchanges
No desires; its thought loves what hope
     estranges."

Such need may see reason, the perfect real—
A body ready as love's steady token
Fed thought unbroken as pleasure induces—
True to thought wearies never its ideal
That loves love, head, every eddy. Broken
Plea, best unspoken, a lip's change produces
Suffers to confuse this thought and its loci,
The foci of things timelessly reflected—
Substance subjected to no human prevision,
Free as exists it loves: worms dig; imprecision
Of indignation cannot make the rose high
Or close sigh, therein blessedness effected
Thru power has directed love to envision
Where body is it bears a like decision.

Love speaks: "in wracked cities there is less
     action,
Sweet alyssum sometimes is not of time; now
Weep, love's heir, rhyme now how song's
     exaction
Is your distraction—related is equated,
How else is love's distance approximated."

   Zukofsky's greatest gift lies in transmuting events into po-
etry. The thing as it happens. The how of it happening becomes
the poem's form. "A"—10's "Paris/ Of your beautiful phrases/ Is
fallen/ The wire service halted/ *Go ahead Paris.*" In this movement
Zukofsky meets a particular kind of scourge with a power of his
own:

   The Rhino is a lovely beast
   He has two horns or one at least
   And neither horn is just a horn

Provoking a dictator's scorn
His surest backside venting scorn
He sits upon the Rhino's horn
And corporate spumes up a yeast
The Rhino such a lovely beast

Empaled beneath the Rhino's knee
People foul in its wet majesty
It feels them with a heavy paw
The spittle dribbles from its jaw
He mires their bleeding overalls
The loveliest of animals

He has also handled the A-bomb tests which demonstrators on the spot tell us are "beautiful, relax and enjoy em . . . the greatest show on earth."

Journeyed. Home. "A"—11, probably the high mark of all "A" so far in construction, subject matter and emotion of intellect, starts with the prelude:

River that must turn full after I stop dying
Song, my song, raise grief to music
Light as my loves' thought, the few sick
So sick of wrangling: thus weeping,
Sounds of light, stay in her keeping
And my son's face—this much for honor.

The whole poem—Bach's *Passion* continues in the last stanza:

His voice in me, the river's turn that finds the
Grace in you, four notes first too full for talk,
    leaf
Lighting stem, stems bound to the branch that
    binds the
Tree, and then as from the same root we talk,
    leaf
After leaf of your mind's music, page, walk leaf
Over leaf of his thought, sounding
His happiness: song sounding
The grace that comes from knowing
Things, her love our own showing
Her love in all her honor.'

The Twelfth Movement—the longest—stops at the half-way mark. He tells us somewhere along toward the end of it:

> I've finished 12 "books"
> So to speak,
> Of 24—
> A kind of childlike
> Play this division
> Into 24,

Here we have Aristotle, Spinoza, Celia, Paul—grandfather and grandson, Ovid, Shakespeare. Zukofsky has been intrigued for some time by an Ovid-Shakespeare-Spinoza continuum. According to his essay *Bottom* (New Directions 14) which is the beginning of a book on Shakespeare, both the Bard and Spinoza looked up to Ovid, and thirty-five years after the publication of the First Folio Spinoza had abstracted Shakespeare's drama. "*A*"—12 says this too, and much else—notably Lucretius as the creator of Hotspur might have read him, a chart of learning to be taken lightly (sic), Paracelsus (without Browning's fuss), a graph of Plato and an integration of actual present-day letters. Editors have spoken of its length—85 pages—as though we live by page numbers. "— Look, Paul, where/ The sawhorses of "*A*"—7/ have brought me."

> *Out of deep need*
> Four trombones and the organ in the nave
> A torch surged—
> Timed the theme Bach's name,
> Dark, larch and ridge, night:
> From my body to other bodies
> Angel and bastards interchangeably
> Who had better sing and tell stories
> Before all will be abstracted.
> So goes: first, *shape*
> The creation—
> A mist from the earth,
> The whole face of the ground;
> Then *rhythm*—
> And breathed breath of life;
> Then *style*—
> That from the eye its function takes—
> "Taste" we say—a living soul.

"I'm an artist," said six-year-old Paul. "I'll do what I want/
The violin in the morning,/ a mister of arts,/ a red fire in a blue
fog at night/ in the afternoon paint."

> At a certain age the child cries about
> His right to handle a gadget
> Or a system for flushing one's water.
> As I said one night impatiently to Paul
> Who had waked me, and forgetting
> I hurried, lèse majesté, to flush
> —Crying about flushed p?

Paracelsus:

> Again, again
> Despised
> By the pack that is large,
> Whose understanding and art are small—
> My father, who's never forsaken me
> Died and I buried him.

And the blessed:

> Hate
> When loved
> Becomes
> Love,
> But it's true
> No one
> Wants
> To be sick
> To get well.
> The way
> Things are,
> Quiet
> Is happier
> Than most words.

As the world continues, the poem is whirled into liveforever.
Aside from the fact that Zukofsky's short poems are intensely

individual and their energy sings in a new way, they move in a circular path "so that we may think in our time." Indeed they seem to move in all directions at once—each of the smallest and the most quiet a field of magnetic force. The subject matter of *55 Poems* (1941) is various—the young man excited by what he sees around him. One day as he was riding the subway to work an insect which he found to be the preying mantis perched on him, opening its mouth. The thing worked itself into the poem "Mantis" with a poem interpreting "Mantis." The "Interpretation" asks what form should "Mantis" take?

> That this thought's torsion
> Is really a sestina
> Carrying subconsciously
> Many intellectual and sensual properties of the
> forgetting
> and remembering Head
> One human's intuitive Head

> Dante's rubric
> Incipit
> Surrealiste
> Re-collection

> A twisted shoe by a pen, an insect, lost,
> "To the short day and the great sweep of
> shadow."

"Wicker-work—/ As a force, one would lie to one's feelings not to use it."

> One feels in fact inevitably
> About the coincidence of the mantis lost in the
> subway,
> About the growing oppression of the poor—
> Which is the situation most pertinent to us—,
> With the fact of the sestina:
> Which together fatally crop up again
> To twist themselves anew
> o

The word sestina has been
Taken out of the original title. It is no use
                    (killing oneself?)
            —Our world will not stand it,
                the implication of a too regular form.

        ○

There should be today no use for a description
        of it
Only for a "movement" emphasizing its use,
        since it's

                            been around,

    An accident in the twisting
    Of many and diverse "thoughts"
    I.e. nerves, glandular facilities, electrical cranial
        charges

Never subduing "The longing for touch to an idea."
    Among the songs in 55 is at least one so tightly evolved that
we see it now as a precursor of a style that may point the future
for Zukofsky and others highly sensitized, viz. "who endure days
like this." Ten years later (1950) the tension finds a simpler equa-
tion:

                    And without
            Spring it is spring why
            Is it death here grass somewhere
            As dead as lonely walks
            As living has less thought that is
                    The spring.

            Spring it is spring why
            Is it death grass somewhere
            As dead as walks
            As living has less thought that is
            A spring. And without.

In much the same cyclic form appear these of 1953:

_____

With
a Valentine
(the 12 February)

Hear, her
Clear
Mirror,
Care
His error.
In her
Care
Is clear.

With a Valentine
(The 14 February)

Hear her
(Clear mirror)
Care.
His error.
In her care—
Is clear.

Hear, her
Clear
Mirror,
Care
His error.
In her,
Care
Is clear.

Hear her
Clear mirror
Care his error
In her care
Is clear

Hear
Her
Clear
Mirror
Care

His
Error in
Her
Care
Is clear

Hear
Her
Clear,
Mirror,
Care
His
Error in
Her—
Care
Is
Clear.

"The 12 February" saying the opposite of Lord Herbert's "In a Glass Window for Inconstancy," but "The 14 February" perhaps a 20th century prayer: at any rate to the poet useful as object of movement and speech.

Multiple interests, poetry following an order of speech, new ideas generating new metrics—these are by now fairly well accepted criteria unless at times there is still "too much air in the air." There is also the dictum to mean exactly what you mean. Poets who reach out ahead of readers necessarily find themselves called obscure. A current of reality always exists in Zukofsky even if involved. It is one of his own tenets that "The emotional quality of good poetry is founded on exact observation" (*A Test of Poetry*, Routledge & Kegan Paul, Ltd., London, 1952). *Anew* (1946) contains the lovely, minutely in-wreathed flowering of Zukofsky's poetic genius. The poems are at once objective and intimate, written, many of them, for members of the family and for friends— sent to friends on postcards or valentines—the years' greetings whose forms are completed by Celia Zukofsky's music. All of these are more or less subject to the order of Mozart's "poetry must be the obedient daughter of music."

Anew 24:

The men in the kitchens
Their women in the foundries
The children in the wars
The old men at the boundaries.

Anew 40, "Celia's birthday poem":

> No ache, love's the way to start the New Year,—
> chant then, "New Year" like "No ache" in your ear,
> all the while I praise wind and love your face
> above snow that melts over trees thru space:
> carol "No ache" like "New Year" between trees
> that removed still share a few centuries.

There are uncollected poems about little wrists and mittens and this:

> Hello, little leaves,
> Said not St. Francis
> But my son in the spring,
> Doing at two
> (Neither really begged)
> What it took the other—
> He'd agree and laugh—
> 44 years to do.

With *Anew* we are given a sense of the perpetually active, as love is. William Carlos Williams has said, "This book is brilliant through an over-all consciousness of its own warmth, its own despairs, its own excellence in the writing. It is happy, happy of a welcoming warmth. That is one of its subtlest and most obvious successes—its serenity in love. For by knowing how to write Zukofsky has found it possible again to express love. You cannot express anything unless you invent how to express it. A poem is not a freudian 'escape' (what childlishness) but an adult release to knowledge, in the most practical, engineering manner."

Sounding out pretty much all of life, the first note of the fugue is present when the last note is struck.

> And so till we have died
> And grass with grass
> Lie faceless as the grass
>
> Grow sheathed with the grass.
> Between our spines a hollow
> The stillest sense will pass
> Or weighted cloud will fol-
> low. (*Anew* 19)

o

The Poetry of Cid Corman

In Bashō's day, poems were left on posts. Today—and not surprisingly Japan-associated—we come upon several solitary posts—nine books in six years, poems rare and at the same time numerous, by the one author, Cid Corman. He is also editor of the poetry journal *Origin*, his present home Kyoto.

Corman is the poet of quiet. "Each man an empire when he enters/a silence." And again: "There are things to be said. But to whom tell/the silences?" They're told but he's careful—o he's suspicious as the devil of too many words. Of thought, even—

The fabric

downstairs as
I look in
from the street

I can catch
the loom and
can sense the

heartbeat
strengthen the
night coming

"Not to have thought through/anything and yet/only through this day/to have thought at all."
Poems precise, plain and sweet—

At day's end
child asleep
in his arms

he steps light—
her bonnet
on his head.

And

The Offerings

Too many things on the altar.
A petal would do.
Or the ant that stops for a moment at it.

Reminds one of Williams' "The Red Wheelbarrow"? To add to
"The Offerings" would be to hold up an extra finger as Bashō said
when he found the perfect poem. *All in All*, which contains this
Corman poem, is in format and contents—a large book with
drawings (illuminations) by Hidetaka Ohno—one of the most
beautiful books of our time.

Short poems on large subjects: Wonder, Contentment. But
solid. "Either you are here/or you're not. And/if you are, this is
the place to stand"—

I picked a
leaf up

it weighed
my vision

I knelt and
placed it

almost
where it was

"to contemplate/contentment"—

Tea in the green fields
served by a monk, green
tea, all that he has.

Through the light thatched roof
the sky gets in and
at the edges more.

In fact, "One gets/to care less for all/save downright good feel-
ing"—

The rain steadies
wisdom. After
the silences

are drummed out, from
the wild depths of
the heart the one

native hears truth.
He emerges
in the sun light.

And "hands clap/invoking warmth/beating time to/a slow snow."

Little still states. World news: sun on the sill; a bug: "A black
and gold beetle/weighs a grass/to whose end it walks"; the rain
gathering at the end of the pine needle "in sudden water-buds
that/as suddenly descent"; a friend who is quiet:

The hand that I hold to the light
fills. What more do I offer you,
my love, than what the light gives?

Use what there is, the poet tells himself, "the mystery of the
simple seeing." Express suspense. Express *listen!*—

rain stops
night knows when
to listen

what falls
glistens now
in the ear

In Corman country there is no violence or hate.

Bashō's concern was to publish very little, Cid Corman's to
publish and let the leaf stay where it falls. Let those read with joy
who are worthy. And another year more leaves come into being.

Books by Corman: *Nonce* (The Elizabeth Press, 103 Van Et-
ten Blvd., New Rochelle, N.Y., 1965). *A Table in Provence* is ob-

tainable from Laurence McGilvery, THE NEXUS, 780 Prospect, La Jolla, California 92037, as are the following: *in no time, for good, Sun Rock Man, in good time, the Descent from Daimonji, for instance, All in All.*

Notes

LEGEND

The following abbreviations appear in the notes:

LN   Lorine Niedecker

NG   *New Goose*. Prairie City, Illinois: Press of James A. Decker, 1946.

MF   *My Friend Tree*. Edinburgh, Scotland: Wild Hawthorn Press, 1961.

NC   *North Central*. London: Fulcrum Press, 1968.

T&G   *T&G*. Penland, North Carolina: Jargon Society, 1969.

LW   *My Life By Water: Collected Poems 1936–1968*. London: Fulcrum Press, 1970.

EA   "Earth and Its Atmosphere"

"Wasted Energy." First appeared in LN's high school yearbook, *The Tchogeerrah* for 1922, p. 98. The poem was reprinted in *Origin*, fourth series, No. 16 (July 1981), 1–2.

"Mourning Dove" appeared in *Parnassus: A Wee Magazine of Verse*, II, 2 (15 November 1928), 4.

When "Transition" first appeared in *The Will-O-The Wisp*, III, 3 (September/October 1928), n.pag., the first line read "Colours of October."

"Spirals." First appeared in *Poetry*, XLII, 6 (September 1933), 308–309.

"Mother Geese." First appeared in *New Directions in Prose and Poetry*, ed. James Laughlin, IV (Norfolk, CT.: New Directions, 1936), n.pag. The sequence contains the poem beginning "There's a better shine," which appeared in Louis Zukofsky, *A Test of Poetry* (New York: The Objectivist Press, 1948, p. 41), NG, FT, T&G, and LW. In LW the punctuation between the final two lines is: . . . ., or two dots on either side of a space.

    There is a manuscript version of the sequence under the title, "Mother Goose," with the following contents: "O let's glee glow as we go," "She had tumult of the brain," "Troubles to win," "A country's economics sick," and "There's a better shine." The texts of the variant poems are:

> Troubles to win
> and battles to bin
> and after
> a tear in the side
> of all my ties
>   and barn
>   dances.

A country's economics sick
affects its people's speech

No bread and cheese and strawberries
I have to pay, they say.

Till in revolution rises
the strength to change

the undigestible phrase.

The poem beginning "My coat threadbare" was reprinted as a separate poem in NG, T&G, and LW. In LW the second line reads: "over and down Capital Hill."

"Fascist Festival." There is a manuscript version of the sequence with the following contents: "The music lady," "Jim Poor's his name," "Scuttle up the workshop," "There was a bridge once that said I'm going," "When do we live again Ann," "Missus Dorra," "No retiring summer stroke." The texts of the variant poems are:

Jim Poor's his name
and Poor Jay's mine
his hair's aflame
not worth a dime
         or he'd sell it.
  o

Scuttle up the workshop
Settle down the dew
I'll tell you what my name is
When we've made the world new.
  o

There was a bridge once that said I'm going
and a cistern that said What Ho
and the stick said lying on the ground
how am I to grow?
  o

When do we live again, Ann
when dirt flies high
in wheeling time
and the lights of their eyes see ours.
For if it's true
and they the flowers
from stock that's running out
they need to be planted over.

They'll never know
the weeping difference, Ann
when the whole world laughs again.
  o

No retiring summer stroke
nor the dangerous parasol
on the following sands
no earth under fire flood lava forecast,
not the pop play of tax, borrow or inflate
but radiant, tight energy
boring from within
communizing fear
into stroke,
work.
o

The first poem of this sequence, "The music, lady," was reprinted as a separate poem in NG.

"News," and "Will You Write Me A Christmas Poem" appear only in manuscript. A note on the manuscript page of "News" reads: "I first had as first line Your wit, the lover said. Maybe *To Wit* shd be title and leave out the lover said since I'm no longer in depression."

"Black Hawk held." In EA there is no comma after "away" at the end of the third line.

"Remember my little granite pail?" In NG there was an exclamation point and not a dash at the end of the third line.

"Ash woods, willows close to shore." The text here is from EA. The poem was printed in NG, T&G, and BC. In the other appearances the second and third lines of the final stanza read: "till he lost his spring and fall; / if he could say: trees carved for—[.]"

"Mr. Van Ess bought 14 washcloths?" In NG "14" appeared as "fourteen." In NG the fourth line of the first stanza reads: "to the Methodist church, I guess."

"Asa Gray wrote Increase Mather." In a letter to Louis Zukofsky dated "Tuesday"[early 1959] LN added a stanza which comes before the present one of "Asa Gray wrote Increase Lapham." It reads:

Great grass! The shoots Michaux
    brought back to Philadelphia
by way of Bartram and Linne
    bear Jefferson's name.

The poem was entitled "Great grass," and LN wanted the two stanza poem to be included in FT.

"Not feeling well." As printed in NG, FT, and T&G, the internal margins were considerably different. The margins and spacing here are that of EA.

"I wrote another" appears in a letter to Louis Zukofsky dated 1 February 1959. LN wrote, "On udder(sic) side I use your words and copy out thus." The poem derives from Zukofsky's poem "Homage," the second one in the collection *I's (pronounced eyes)*, which begins:

> Homage
>
> Of love for, to
> the young

"Grampa's got his old age pension." In NG there was no dollar sign at the beginning of the second line.

"A working man appeared in the street." This poem first appeared in *Furioso: A Magazine of Verse*, I, 1 (Summer 1939), 5.

"van Gogh." In LW the title was "Van Gogh." In NG the the first line reads: "I have at times to sit in the dunes." In LW the fourth line reads, "Is like a desert . . . the family's shoes."

"Pioneers." The spacing and internal margins here are accepted from LW. There are considerable differences in both in the previous appearances in NG and T&G. In EA the first section of the poem has been discarded, so the the whole poem, untitled, consists of the eleven lines beginning "Between fighting fourteen nation's invading troops" and ending with "swayed back and forth from lack of food." In NG the third line from the end reads: "lecturing on Einstein—[.]"

"(L.Z.)." The manuscript bears the notation "Lorine 1945."

"New." The manuscript bears the notation "Final version Nov 22/45." "Old man who seined." This poem was part of a sequence entitled "In Exchange for Haiku" when it first appeared in *Neon*, 4 (1959), [5]. The internal margin for the penultimate line in FT is at the space between "dipnet" and "shape" in the line above.

"You are my friend." The text of this poem appeared in FT, T&G and LW. There is a typescript dated "Jan 20, 1961" as being received by Zukofsky, but previous to that there is a signed version dated as being received "Sept 15/60," which reads:

> Why do I press it: are you my friend?
> You bring me peaches
> and the high bush cranberry
>   you carry
> my fishpole
>
> you water my worms
> you patched my boot
> with your mending kit
>   nothing in it
> but my hand

The trouble of the boot on you, friend
your dentist fingers
an orchard to mow
you also
paint

The text of the poem was arrived at later than the other poem in this section, but its position was established by the ordering of LW and is so kept in its position.

"Dear Paul" 1. The text for the first version of "For Paul" has been taken from the manuscript "For Paul and Other Poems." Notes on the manuscript indicate that the final copy was received by Louis Zukofsky 12 Dec. 1957. Differences between the early and later manuscript are slight, but have been noted. The Paul of the poems is Paul Zukofsky.

In no other document does Niedecker refer to the "groups" as parts. The 1957 manuscript has the typed heading "Part V," which follows the pattern of numbering in the parts of the published and unpublished groups. This poem is not the missing "Group 5," therefore. In addition, all other "Groups" have more than one poem, while this one is a single poem. Conceivably this part could belong within a separate group of other poems. Niedecker was meticulous about the titles and groupings of her poems, so would not have mislabled a part for a group.

In earlier typescript line five begins: "He can say[.]"

In earlier manuscript line 67 reads "Dennie" and not "Reggy's[.]"

Lines 129–134, "The elegant office girl" to "half-pulled" do not appear in earlier typescript.

Line 140 in earlier typescript reads "John Sebastian brook" in the place of "John Sebastian Brook[.]"

A two line stanza reading "Put that in your Opus/ 5 f's for forte" appears in the earlier typescript after line 182, "yours will still be hot[.]"

"Dear Paul" 2. *Quarterly Review of Literature*, VIII, 2 (1955), 117–119.

"Dear Paul" 3. from LW. In the version from LW, line 17, "if there were no marsh or stream," has been added after the appearance of the poem in T&G.

"Dear Paul":[4] This final version is from a late typescript prepared by LN, entitled "The Earth and Its Atmosphere."

FOR PAUL. The sequence "For Paul" exists in seven sequences. "Group Five" in LN's ordering is not present. Individual poems are repeated, but not always in the same order; and different poems appear in different sequences. Some poems also appear within the present volume in the sequences, and as separate poems. There is a manuscript typescript entitled "For Paul and Other Poems." The note, "Final copy sent Nov 20 49" appears at the bottom of the first page of the text.

Group One, without that identification, appeared in *New Directions in Prose and Poetry 12*, ed. James Laughlin (New York: New Directions, 1950), 181–185.

is the text presented here. Where the published text differs from the manuscript, notes have been added.

In poem VII, there was no break between the second and third stanza. Another version of the poem, received by Zukofsky 1 March 1950 reads:

> The young ones go away to school
> come home to moon
>
> Like Frederick the Great
> what was it he ate
> that had to be sown in the dark of the moon
>
> Looking for rain?
> Wait for the moon to change
>
> But Edwin—Edwin's glorious—
> runs all over his acres without a hat
> as though he knew—
>   the moon
> changes every day!

Poem IX. When the poem was printed in LW the first eight lines were deleted, and the six lines beginning "Hi, Hot-and-Humid" were printed as a separate poem.

Group Two: The continuation of the sequence, designated "Group Two," appeared in *The New Mexico Quarterly*, XXI, 2 (Summer 1951), 205–211. A prefacing note by the editor reads in part: "The long poem *For Paul* is a work in progress. The central figure is a child of six or seven who composes music and plays the violin. Like other children, he is discovering the world around him each day, confronting its real strangeness and answering it with the play fantasy which is every child's resource."

Poem XI. The manuscript version contains the following lines:

> Oh yes, you're from the country
> called the Source.
>   Trees and stars?
> Of course, if they console you.
>   Would the nurse in your plant
>   give me sweet pills?
> No! We're not at war.
>   One constellation is:
>   we can always play
>   Ask for a job.

"One console-ation is" appears at the right in LN's hand, with the hyphen appearing as a blackened space. The following typed note appears at the bottom: "(constellation simply a child's mispronunciation of consolation—you don't get that? Believe I'd like Trees and stars? Of course, if they console you taken out. Those were additions. You unders and Diddy is the speaker on the right side??)"

Line twelve of the typescript, after the line Trees and stars?, has been deleted. It is: "Of course, if they console you."

Poem XII. An earlier typescript contains the following note: "(Industrial relations and business weren't all he knew, that's my meaning. But if the above doesn't do it, put Business in place of industrial relations. How involved can you make this?—are *you* the lawyer-poet?) I've put back say and said—you don't condense this kind of thing—it's for either this or nothing. These on this page [Poems XII and XIII] I hadn't intended for For Paul but now I don't know—Blues song and both springing out of looking for a job—what do you think?" Poem XII in an earlier version was entitled "Office Blues." The manuscript page containing poems XII and XIII is dated as being received by Zukofsky 30 Dec. 1950.

Poem XIII. "He moved in light[.]" This poem appeared as a separate poem in T&G and LW.

Poem XIV. The following lines appear at the bottom of the page as alternatives to lines two and three:

> the glow of contemplation
> in our time
> along this road

Poem XIV. appears as a separate poem in LW, p. 61. Line 6 in the typescript reads "right down among 'em[.]"

Poem XV. The following lines appear at the bottom of the page as alternatives to the final stanza of the poem:

> Dear fiddler: how'll you carry
> a counter that sings
> counter to sense
>   in the presence
> of man's stings?

In a letter to Zukofsky, dated as being received 30 Dec. 1956, LN wrote: "I figure the Lugubre for a child to take the place of the somewhat crazy You have power politics, Paul."

There is another poem in manuscript dated as being received by Zukofsky 16 Jan. 1951 designated as "to follow XV."

> He asked: Will man obsolesce
> when he sends the rays against himself?
> And she, sore pressed: Absurd!—
> obsolesce is not a word.

> But think of Troy, it was a word
> before we dug and found the world
> so go up in a kite.
> Still, could she be right?

The note in the bottom corner reads: "(subject to change as per yr letter I've not yet rcd.)"

Poem XVI, "Tell me a story about the last war." This poem appeared as a separate poem in T&G and LW, and also in manuscript.

line 3: in NMQ appearance "marshal" appeared as "Marshal."

lines 4–5: in NMQ appearance there was a period after "flatter" and "but" appeared as "But." In T&G, LW and the manuscript these features do not appear.

Poem XVII, "I'd like to tell you about a man" exists as a longer poem in manuscript, "He was here before the wild swans died out," and as the printed poem "Thure Kumlien." Both are presented later in this volume. The second version of the poem, in manuscript, contains the notation "earlier draft than 18 Jan 1951" in Zukofsky's hand. There is another draft closer to the printed draft that is marked as being received by Zukofsky 18 Jan 1951. In all cases, it was LN's habit to condense not expand lines. The second version, therefore, must be the first draft of the poem, and the notes must be in error. The following differences between the printed poem and the second draft are noted:

lines 3–4:	He was there while the wild swans
	were still afloat. Bigwigs wrote
lines 15–16:	"And gathered around the first lamp—
	kerosene—how we shone."
lines 17–24:	For Thure The Solitary Tattler, Wilson's Phalarope.
	He exchanged dried New England plants
	for those around his home
	at Koshkonong. One day he found
	an astor down in the ditch
	by the old turnpike—to it he gave
	his name as tho he were rich.

In the left margin appear the following lines in LN's hand, which became lines 18–20 in the published poem:

> opened a door
> to learned birds
> with their latest books
> who walked New England
> shore[.]

In the left margin appear the following lines in LN's hand, which became lines 21–23 in the published poem:

> one day by the old turnpike still
> the marsh, down in the ditch
> he found a new astor to it he gave

Lines 25–29 appear as:

> The trouble with war for a botanist—
> he daren't drop out of the line
> of March to examine a flower—he can only
> hope to come back sometime,
> or now in power wars when half
> the world is shell-burst
> observe a sky-exotic
> attract a bomber-bird

The following note appears at the bottom of the manuscript page: "I did better on an ode to Koshkonong in high school. Unless you insist I won't use it. Second stanza might be omitted and third begin: He saw The Solitary Tattler "is it ever white"—they changed color as do herons and egrets in various stages of growth in various sections of country as they fly up this way from Florida.

Poem XVIII. "Shut up in the woods[.]" This poem appeared as a separate poem in manuscript, T&G, LW, and EA. In those three appearances there were no quotation marks as in the appearance in NMQ. In that appearance there were quotation marks around the first sentence, the second stanza, and the third and fourth stanza. In the NMQ a comma appeared after "gently" at the end of the third line. In the other appearances a colon was used.

Poem XIX. Appears as a separate poem in T&G, and LW, p. 72. In the typescript there is no stanza break after line 5, and there are three dots, indicating a stanza break as a separation of the text, after the second stanza, which contains the additional lines:

> you were right.
> Happy New Year[.]

An earlier manuscript contained the following note:
"Happy New Year—as I hear it sung there is slight pause after bitter and so winter brotherhood comes together—these phrases that look forward and back are fascinating to do but I suppose there's a limit. Trees could have apostrophe after it[.] [W]hat started the whole thing aside from 'better than bitter' was an inversion with sorrow clean[.] [S]illy? We still get out deepest feels of [in hand, can not read.]" See version from LW later in this volume.

Group Three. This group of poems was marked "Final Copy Sent Sept 27/51."

Poem II. "What horror to awake at night[.]" This poem appeared as a separate poem in manuscript, T&G, LW.

Poems VI and VII. "Jesse James and his brother Frank" and "May you have lumps in your mashed potatoes[.]" In the manuscript the two poems were numbered as separate poems, while in T&G and LW they appear as a single poem with three dots separating them. In EA only the second poem is present. When "May you have lumps" appeared in *Origin*, second series, 2 (July 1961), 28, the second line read: "Henry and William cried[.]"

Group Four. Poem I. "Sorrow moves in wide waves[.]" In manuscript the poem appears as the first two stanzas only, and with the notation "(after Henry James)" after and below the final line. "Old Mother" (the last two stanzas) appeared as a separate poem in *Origin*, second series, 2 (July 1961), 28. In T&G and LW the poem is again divided into two poems. In T&G the notation "HJ" appears before the first poem. The version of the manuscript is here retained to note the movement of the sequence. "What horror to awake at night" appears in a letter, dated as being received by Zukofsky 29 Sept 1951. The following comments precede the poem: "Characteristically after writing a postcard I decide to enlarge. Only a 3 decker from the middle of the night, rather, two from there, then the third from the next afternoon which began to have a wink in it (thinking of Diddy spotting a canary instead of practicing."

Poem III. "The shining brown steel casket[.]" This poem was revised and reprinted in T&G and LW as "Dead/she now lay deaf to death[.]" It is reprinted from those sources separately later in this collection.

Poem IV. "Two old men[.]" This poem appeared as a separate poem in T&G and LW.

Poem VII. "Can knowledge be conveyed that isn't felt?" This poem appeared as a separate poem in a previous manuscript.

Group Six. Poem I. "Ten O'clock[.]" This poem appeared in a separate manuscript as only a three stanza poem. The manuscript is noted as being received by Zukofsky 22 Oct 1952.

Poems II, III, IV. In a previous manuscript these poems appear under the general title "Adirondack Summer."

Poem III. "The slip of a girl-announcer" appears in a post card to Zukofsky dated 12 Aug. 1952. Preceding the poem the following comments appear: "Your letter is TERRIFIC—enchanting, impossible, impassable, incomparable—I've read it three times and I'm still shaking with chuckles. It prompts me to descend practically to doggerell." The second stanza of the poem read:

> A saxy age
> and Bach, you see, is in Dakota
> but don't belittle her
> she waits to lend her motor.

Group Seven. Poem I. "My father said 'I remember[.]'" In the manuscript appearance the first line read: "My father: I remember[.]" The poem, without the final three lines presented here, was reprinted as a separate poem in T&G with the present first line, and without the quotation marks in the first and final lines. It was reprinted with the quotation marks—the text presented here—in LW.

Poem IV. "In Europe they grow a new bean while here[.]" The typescript, marked as "Final version" received 1 Dec 1951 is enough different to be cited in full:

In Russia they grow a new bean while here
                we tie bundles of grass
with strands of itself as they used to American grain,
                against the cold blast

around my house, my neighbor: Do yet in Russia I guess.

From his sister in Maine: We've found a nice warm place
                (in the hay?)
for the winter. Charlie sleeps late, I'm glad for his sake,
                it shortens his day

Around my house the old bean in America yet.

An earlier version of the poem contained the following line as the final one, with the present line as an alternative: "Around my house in America yet." A note addressed, dated 1/29/55, to Zukofsky reads: "(I change Russia, the word, to Europe, and you sent out 'A'–8."

    Poem [V]. The manuscript evidence for the inclusion of this poem as the fifth poem of the sequence is ambiguous. It appears with the other poems but is not numbered in sequence. It has a thematic place in the sequence, so it is included here.

Group Eight. Poem I. "Paul/ when the leaves/ fall[.]" This poem was reprinted as a separate poem with the present text in T&G and LW. A final selection of poems for this group was not made, so alternative poems IV and V have been included.

    Poem II. "To Aeneas who closed his piano[.]" This poem was reprinted in T&G and LW. In T&G "Aeneas" appeared as "AEneas." The poem appears in a typescript, dated Oct. 5, 1953, with the following note: "(Was amazed and delighted to find it fell into stanzas and with end rhymes (as over). Do you like this block or the other (over)?[not clear what poem LN is referring to here.] AEneas is a Greek Catholic name. The McA's say Anis but if they're spelling it AEneas as they do, I suppose it ought to be pronounced Eeneas? If I keep this FOR PAUL I might use Enos instead?)" A note on the poem in Group Eight, dated as being received 1 Dec. 1953, reads: "Chopin got sick in Majorca and had that terrible journey home. I've tried everything: the rough sea journey etc. but always come back to original. I may omit III."

    Poem IV. "So you're married, you man," appears as Poem IV and as Poem VI in a condensed form. In an earlier manuscript the following two stanzas appear after the first two of the present text, followed by the final two:

You'll find the same man's
got two jobs—he must give
all the things to his wife
she demands but why live

if you can't take time
to be home from this grave
or you do and your wife's out
with another slave.

Poem V. "'Oh ivy green[.]" This poem appears in different versions as Poem V and also as Poem VIII in this sequence. There is an additional variant of the poem:

> "Oh ivy green
>   oh ivy green—
> you spoke your poem
> as we walked a city terrace
> and said if you could hear
>   —sneeze
> sneeze on the corner—
>   Handel clean
> Christmas would be cherished
>
> Christmas would be cherished
>
> To the mother
>   color
> does not matter
> with her son's cold
> no better
>   unless
>   a friend should tender
> rest and hold
> her warm till winter's old
>   warm till winter's old

LN holograph notes on the manuscript indicate the following alternative lines:

line 7	sneeze on the beat—
lines 17–19	"a friend project
	till winter's beat is old
	till winter's beat is old
lines 17–18	her warm in a green robe
	her warm in a green robe

A note at the bottom of the page in LN's hand reads: "I prefer 1st stanza ending with cherished but not the 2nd with old[.]"
Holograph notes on the manuscript for Poem VIII indicate the following alternative lines:

line 7	sneeze on the beat
line 10	"cherished" to replace "green"
line 15	a friend project
lines 17–18	warmth in winter measure
	warmth in winter measure

Poem IV. "The cabin door flew open[.]" A holograph note indicates that the end of the line could read "generally happy[.]"
Poem V. "My friend the black and white collie[.]" This poem appears in a separate typescript with the following note: "Would kind of like this as number

V, between you're married and "Oh ivy green"—if you think so keep the clip on, otherwise trow[sic] it away—"

    Poem VI. "So you're married, young man[.]" See notes for Poem IV.

    Poem VIII. "'Oh ivy green'[.] See notes for Poem V.

"You have power politics, Paul[.]" Holograph markings indicate the following alternatives:

line 6	let a song, a fall
line 13	In still later states
line 17	and man must at last obsolesce

"He was here before the wild white swans died out" and "Thure Kumlien" see note to Poem XVII in Group 2 of "for Paul." The manuscript for "He was here" is dated as being received by Zukofsky 18 Jan 1951.

"To print poems" appears in a letter to Zukofsky, dated as being received 14 Dec. 1956. Preceding the poem, LN made the following comments: "Well drilling commences soon into which as I guess I said I sink around $700. What would $300 for printing amount to after that, even without a job??? I've hurriedly entered in my journal:"

"Sorrow moves in wide waves" and "Old Mother turns blue and from us." See note in "For Paul" Group IV, Poem 1.

"Happy New Year." See note "For Paul" Group II, Poem XIX.

"Horse, hello." When this poem appeared in *New Directions in Prose & Poetry 12*, ed. James Laughlin (New York: New Directions, 1950), p. 186, it was entitled "Poem." That was probably an editorial attribution, since in all other appearances the poem did not have that title. The text in manuscript, dated as received by Zukofsky "June 25/49" differs from the present text enough to be cited:

>   Horse, hello
> I too live hot before the final flash,
> cavort for others' gain. We toss our shining heads
> in an ever increasing standard of sweet.
> The mind deranged, Democritus. Who knows us, friend?—
> our indicator needles shot off scale—
> Spinoza, Burns, Xenophanes knew us
> in days when thought arose and kindly stayed . . .
> all creatures whatsoever desire this glow.

"Energy glows at the lips." This is the full text as it was first printed in *New Directions in Prose & Poetry 12*, ed James Laughlin (New York: New Directions, 1950), pp. 185–186. The text also appears in the typescript "For Paul and Other Poems." When the poem appeared in LW, p. 70, the final stanza was deleted.

"Depression years." The title in the typescript is "Depression ballad."

"What's wrong with marriage." The following note headed the two versions of the poem:

"First version which to MD states the case better than the second but the second is less jingly. Mebbe I shdn't ever have gone to NY to meet the real writer but shd. have stayed in my little tiny country patch and written country ballads to be sung with a *gee*tar! Do I dare use the second version for FOR PAUL with a preference about a banjo or guitar in place of a violin? Of course St. Louis Blues streams through my head and much better thing it is than I cd. do."

"He lives—childhood summers." This poem has been revised more than most of the poem, therefore I have taken the last full text of LW as the one representing the poet's final intention. An earlier typescript reads:

> He lived. He had it—childhood summer
>   thru bare feet
> then years of handling money,
>   silver cold and heat.
>
> Forever the flood—out of it came
>   his wood, dog,
> woman, lost her, daughter—
>   dog paws are warm.
>
> He planted trees, buried carp
>   beneath the rose,
> Saw motion in the stillest
>   as the marsh rail goes.
>
> To bankers on the high land
>   he opened his wine tank
> and sent his only daughter
>   to work in the bank.

The second typescript contains the following differences, and also an additional stanza:

> lines 3–4   then years of handling money's
>   cold and heat
>
> lines 8–9   finish, prologue.
>
>   He planted trees, buried carp
>
> lines 16–17   to work in the bank.

The poem was published in *Golden Goose*, IV, 5 (Oct 1952), 6, and in that appearance contained the following deviations from the final text:

> lines 3–4   the years of handling money's
>   cold and heat
> line 7   daughter,

lines 8–9	finish, prologue.
	He planted trees, buried carp
lines 13–17	he opened his wine tank
	and sent his only daughter
	to work in the bank.

> But he gave her a source
>   to sustain her
> But he gave her a source

"European Travel." The manuscript of this poem is dated "Nov. '45," and contains the following note. "Found this in my notes—no I wouldn't have included it in the book."

"The Element Mother." The first poem in this sequence, "She's Dead," was printed in T&G and LW as "Mother is Dead," while the second was printed as "The Graves." In the typescript, "Earth and its Atmosphere" the title was "The Graves." The third was dropped for publication. "As" in line 4 of "She's Dead" was in lower case in the typescript, but in upper case in T&G and LW. In a manuscript from 1945 "She's Dead" bears the title "The Graves and Other Women."

"Wartime." This is the text of the poem as it appeared in LW. In the manuscript the poem was untitled, had no dash at the end of line 3, a period at the end of line four and a comma at the end of line 5.

"Crèvecoeur." This poem appears in a typescript, undated but from the late 1940s. In later revision the poem becomes "To Paul now old enough to read." There is another shorter version which is part of the manuscript "For Paul and Other Poems" dating from the early 1950s. It is as follows:

> Hero of vegetables, Crèvecoeur
> hero of good
> he learned to know every plant
> in his neighborhood
>
> He loved Nantucket, grazing land
> held in common.
> Here one lawyer only
> found the means to go on.
>
> Green prickly humanity—
> men are plants whose goodness grows
> out of the soil, Mr. Stinkweed
> or Mrs. Rose

> Learn, Crècoeur and learn fast
> and firefly, two pairs of wings
> and a third to read by
> disappearing.

"A Student." In T&G and CP, the obvious error in the third line "of the grass as I mow" has been corrected.

"February almost March bites the cold." The manuscript is marked "Final Copy," and was received by Zukofsky "Mar 19/51." In an earlier version, line 1 reads: "In February almost March I [we] bite the cold." Line 8 reads: "There are no objects here only velocities." Line 11 reads "to move toward May: Give me a care," with "with lupines and" written in above. Line three in the final manuscript has a comma and not a dash at the end of line three.

"We physicians watch the juices rise." The poem is dated as being received by Zukofsky "June 4/52."

"Home." The manuscript page is dated "Jan. 1948." There is an earlier version with the following third stanza:

> no freak is isolate—
> grasses, heron, China,
> days of light:
> Saturday,
> Sunday.

"On hearing the wood pewee. The text here is from LW. When the poem first appeared in *Neon*, 4(1959), [6], the text was somewhat different:

> This is my mew
> as our days in a wild-flying world
> last—
>
> be alone.
> Throw it over—all fashion,
> feud.
>
> Go home where the greenbird
> is—the trees where you pass
> to grass.

In T&G the first four lines are as follows:

> This is my mew
> as our days in a wild-flying world
> last—
>   be alone

"Chimney Sweep." The manuscript is dated "Jan 1948."

"I don't know what wave he's on." The manuscript as received by Zukofsky "Oct. 2/53."

"Yes, my Time's waste." The manuscript was received by Zukofsky "3/10/54."

"In Exchange for Haiku." When the sequence appeared in *Neon*, 4 (1959), [5–6] it was numbered I–V, and contained the following poems: "July, waxwing," "Old man who seined," "People, people," "Linnaeus in Lapland," "Fog-thick morning."

"Springtime's wide." A manuscript version of the poem reads:

> Springtime's
> wide water—
>   yield
>   but the field
> will return

"The soil is poor" and "Michelangelo" appear in the sequence in EA, and so have been added here. The poems are also part of the later sequence "Poems at the Porthole."

The poems from "Fog-thick morning" to "Letter/ of Gerard Manley Hopkins" appeared in the manuscript with poems that finally made up the sequence in LW. They date from 1957–58, and the style and statement of the poems associate them with the published sequence.

Another arrangement of these poems appeared in *Origin*, second series, 2 (July 1961), 27 as a sequence numbered I–V: "Hear/where her snow-grave is," "Springtime's wide," "How white the gulls," "My friend tree," "New-sawed."

"Easter." When the poem appeared in *Origin* second series, 8 (July 1963), there was an additional first line, "Land," and then a stanza break before the text published here.

"Get a load." When the poem appeared in *Origin*, second series, 8 (July 1963), 26, there was no dash at the end of line 3.

"Property is poverty" appears in a typed manuscript attached to a letter dated as being received by Zukofsky 5 June 1962. A holograph note in LN's hand reads "(Don't confuse this with reality—I don't have to foreclose)."

"Now in one year a book" appears in a typed manuscript attached to a letter dated as being received by Zukofsky 5 June 1962, with a different line arrangement:

> Now in one year a book
> published and plumbing
>   took a lifetime to weep
>   a deep
> trickle

"Dusk." In T&G and LW there was a dash after "Dusk" and the second line began "He's." The present text is from EA.

"River-marsh-drowse." The text here is from EA. In T & G and LW the poem ended with a period.

"Letter from Ian." The poem was entitled "Ian's" in *Origin*, third series, 2 (July 1977), 23.

"Sure they drink" and "River-marsh-drowse" appear together in a typescript dated as being received by Zukofsky 19 June 1962.

"Come In." In a manuscript dated "Xmas 1960" the poem was titled "Thanks-giving, Glen Ellyn," and there was a second version.

> Education, kindness
> live here
>
> Whose grandfolk taught:
> work, hard,
> whose dog does not impose
> her long nose
> and barks quietly.
>
> Serious wags its tail
> where white tie-backs expose
> evergreen, green yard.
> Hard
> is lovely here.

The manuscript page from which the final text is taken was received by Zukofsky "Jan 20/61."

"The wild and wavy event." LN wrote the following in a letter to Cid Corman: "You'll see two of the enclosed don't have titles. It strikes me that an editor must wish fervently that his contributors head their poems so that he doesn't have to title all headless poems POEMS. I suppose The wild and wavy event might be called She Watched the Battle of Bunker's Hill and The men leave the car Calla of the Heart-Shaped Leaves or simply Calla."

"Club 26." This poem appeared in *Midwest*, 5/6(Spring 1963), 54, with the title "Place to Dine."

> Our talk, our books
> riled the shore like bullheads
> at the roots of the luscious
> large water lily

Then we entered the lily—
Club 26
built white on a red carpet
quiet
for the massive steak

the circular cool bar
fingers caressing glass stems

We stayed till the stamens trembled.

LN sent the page from the magazine to Zukofsky, which he received 1 April 1963. A note in LN's hand states, "changed to glass stems to caress." A second note states: "This is where we'll have the wedding dinner: Alice Fabian, Al's daughter, husband; George his son & wife Mary McAllister, Robert Reed & Al & neighbors—the man." LN married Albert Millen 24 May 1963.

"The men leave the car." See note for "The wild and wavy event."

"As praiseworthy." When the poem appeared in *Origin*, third series, 2(July 1966), 16, the first line read: "The power of breathing—Epictetus—[.]."

"Watching dancers on ice." When the poem appeared in *Origin*, third series, 2(July 1966), 27, the configuration of lines 3 and 4 was:

the only one
in boots

and the configuration of lines seven and eight was:

he holds her leg
up[.]

"As I paint the street" appeared in *Origin*, third series, 2 (July 1966), 18, with the title "As I Paint the Street."

"Florida." The manuscript was sent to Zukofsky 18 Feb 1962.

"I visit/the graves." The editor has added a comma in the second line for the sake of clarity.

"To foreclose." In a letter to Zukofsky dated as being received 4 Jan. 1963, LN wrote: "Just wrote a poem on foreclosure. Venom against property, the law etc. I invoked Cat 93. (Gregory's 2 lines for 93), the second line changed just enough to suit what I'm talking about. You've got the idea—Latin gets to the roots." In an earlier letter to Zukofsky, dated 24 Dec. 1962, she had written: "you see I now have Gregory's trans. His nice, open, but polite translations." See Horace Gregory, tr. *The Poems of Catullus* (New York: Grove Press, Inc., 1956), p. 159. Poem 93 reads: "I SHALL not raise my hand to please you, Caesar, / nor do I dare if you are white or black."

"In the transcendence." In manuscript the poem had a second stanza:

> I lay down
>   with brilliance
>   I saw a star whistle
> across the sky
>   before dropping off

"The Museum." When the poem appeared in *Origin*, third series, 9 (April 1968), 39 it was the first of a series entitled "Traces of Living Things." The poems in the sequence were: "Museum," "And at the blue ice superior spot," "TV," "Far reach," "Years," "Unsurpassed in beauty," "Human bean," "High class human," "What cause have you," "Stone."

"Far Reach." See note for "The Museum."

"TV." See note for "The Museum."

"What cause have you." See note for "The Museum."

"Laundromat." The text is taken from *Origin*, third series 2(July 1977), 21. In BC the first two lines appeared as:

> Once again a public wedding
> a casual, sudsy

"Unsurpassed in beauty." See note for "The Museum."

"Human Bean." See note for "The Museum."

"High class human." See note for "The Museum."

"Stone." See note for "The Museum."

"The eye." The first version of the poem appeared in *Origin*, third series, 2 (July 1966), 37, while the second is the text from NC, and EA.

"For best work." The text is from a manuscript later than the publication of the poem in *Origin*, third series, (July 1977), 21. In that printing the fourth line "to stand" was aligned directly under "some effort."

"To whom." The text is taken from *Origin*, 2 (July 1966), 26. In BC the first two lines were:

Is there someone
I can leave[.]

"Wild strawberries." The text is taken from *Origin*, third series 2(July 1966), 24.
In BC the text is considerably different:

Ruskin found wild strawberries
and they were a consolation
poor man whose diaries
were grey with instances of rose

I think tonight we'll have the liver
since tomorrow we go out
tho not of course like him
to Metaphysical dinner
following Greco

"Ah your face." When the poem appeared in *Origin*, third series 2 (July 1966),
20, the first line read: "ah, your face—[.].

"J.F. Kennedy after the Bay of Pigs." When the poem appeared in *Origin*, third
series, 7 (October 1967), 53, and NC, the first line read: "To stand up—[.] The
dash was omitted in LW, but has been restored here.

In *Origin*, third series, 7 (October 1967), 53–57, this poem appeared in a
sequence under the heading "Hear and See: eleven poems." The titles in the se-
quence are: "J.F. Kennedy after the Bay of Pigs," "Alone," "Why can't I be
happy," "And what you liked," "Mergansers," "Cleaned all surfaces," "My life/
by water," "'Shelter,'" "You see here," "I walked."

"Lake Superior." In a letter to Cid Corman dated 13 October 1966, LN wrote:
"I've finished the Lake Superior poem—5 pages long—after much culling but I
might just make a small book out of it with a short poem on each page." In
another letter to Cid Corman dated 18 October 1967 LN made the following
comment: "I've taken the Marquette poem out of Traces and put it into the Lake
Superior poem." See note to "The Museum."

"And at the blue ice superior spot." When this poem appeared in NC it had a
first line misplaced from the last line of the previous poem, "Through all the
granite land," "Beauty: impurities in the rock[.]" See note for "The Museum."
LN wrote of the error in letter to Jonathan Williams, dated 4 Feb. 1969: "Em-
barrassment—please use the enclosed Errata notice to drop into your *North Cen-
tral* copy. My God, what next?"

The final typescripts prepared by LN were "Earth and its Armosphere," "Harp-
sicord & Salt Fish," and "The Very Veery,"—subtitled "(Selected from *The Se-
lected Poems*)." The poems printed here are final version, or new versions of older
poems. Poems duplicated earlier in this volume are not reprinted.

"Harpsichord & Salt Fish." This is the final typescript prepared by LN. It consists of the following poems: "Thomas Jefferson," "The Ballad of Basil," "Wilderness," "Consider," "Otherwise," "Nursery Rhyme," "3 Americans," "Poems at the Porthole," "Subliminal," "LZ," "Peace," "Thomas Jefferson Inside," "Foreclosure," "His Carpets Flowered," "Darwin."

"Otherwise." This poem in manuscript was titled "Letter," while in BC it appeared as "Gerard Manley Hopkins."

"Poems at the Porthole." The text here is from a late typescript and is the last arrangement made by LN. When the poems appeared in BC there were four poems: "The soil is poor," "The man of law," "Not all harsh sounds displease—" "Michelangelo." The texts for the second and third poems follow the present sequence. In BC "blue and white" appeared as a separate poem. LN also placed "The soil is poor" and "Michelangelo" in the sequence "In Exchange for Haiku."

"The man of law." The text is taken from a late typescript. The text of the poem in BC is:

> The man of law
>   on the uses
>   of grief
> The poet
>   on the law
>   of the oak leaf

"Subliminal." In BC the poem was untitled, and contained two additional lines at the end of the first section:

>   and my sometimes
> happy fatherphosphor[.]

"waded, watched, warbled" is a separate poem in BC and contained three additional stanzas:

> Faithful to the marsh
> of my childhood
> we camp on the dryest portion
>
> In April's flood-freeze
> crystals hang low on the bush
> all day
> Then green—w're en rapport
> with grass as once or twice
> with humans

"Thomas Jefferson." In a letter to Cid Corman dated 17 March 1970 LN wrote: "I'm embarrassed to ask but the heading up at the right of no. 5 Thomas Jefferson (the Roman temple piece—would you change South of France to The South of France?"

LZ. The typescript for the poem appeared in a letter to Cid Corman dated 1 August 1968. The fifth line in the typescript is was "Test[.]" This was the line when the poem appeared in *Origin*, third series 12 (January 1969), 3.

"Everybody's nose's full." The poem accompanied a letter to Louis Zukofsky, dated as being received 4 Jan. 1963. The beginning of the letter has the following note: "1963 came misting in like the stuff I talk about in enclosed verse." And the following note appears after the typed poem in LN's hand: "A visitation from BP[her father]!! I must be feeling better. No kidding tho, everybody's given em bottle and bottles of air freshner, hair spray, body spray[.] LN is referring to an office party.

"Paean to Place." The poem appeared in LW with different internal margins. The internal margins and spacing in this text are from EA.

"Jefferson and Adams." A note on the manuscript reads, "(not sent out as yet— Jan '70)."

"Prothonotary Warbler." The poet's notes read: "I—Fairly conscious. II is the one I'll probably keep as the one *sleeping under* the other, in large part subconscious. I might have laid an egg (I) tho—?—in any event the egg out of the bird. In II the bird out of the egg and the song before that and the color—

Cather(last two lines of I—you remember she said that in Avignon they know how to live. (That was 1902—wonder what that place is now/)—

Version III—This might be *it*—or is it only fooling around, a kind of Mother Goose warbler?"

"In the hills." The text of this poem appeared in a letter to Cid Corman dated 4 Oct. 1968.

"Bashō." This poem derives from an earlier poem "Alliance."

"The President of the Holding Company" and "Fancy Another Day Gone" appeared in *New Directions in Prose and Poetry*, ed. James Laughlin IV (Norfolk, CT: New Directions, 1936), n.pg.

"Domestic and Unavoidable." The manuscript bears the date 1936.

"As I Lay Dying." The manuscript is dated as being received by Zukofsky 11 January 1952. Page 3A of the manuscript is dated as being received by Zukofsky 28 June. 1952.

"Taste and Tenderness." The manuscript is undated, but was probably written between 1942–1944.

"Uncle" first appeared in *New Directions in Prose and Poetry 1937*, ed. James Laughlin IV (Norfolk, CT: New Directions, 1937), n.pag.

"Stage Directions." The manuscript is dated August 1934.

"The History of Old Abe the War Eagle." The manuscript is dated by Zukofsky as being received Nov. 1940.

[Untitled]. The manuscript is dated 1951.

"Switchboard Girl" first appeared in *New Directions in Prose & Poetry 13*, ed. James Laughlin (New York: New Directions, 1951), 87–89.

This is the text of the review of Zukofsky's *A Test of Poetry* that appeared in a typescript, not the edited text that appeared in *Capital Time* for 18 December 1948. The editor of the Section "Books of Today" was August Derleth.

"The Poetry of Louis Zukofsky" appeared in *Quarterly Review of Literature*, VIII, 3 (1955), 198–210.

"The Poetry of Cid Corman" appeared in *Arts in Society*, III, 4 (Summer 1966), 558–560.

FROM THIS CONDENSERY consists of 2500 copies in cloth, plus 100 copies of a Patrons' Edition, bound in full leather, signed by the Editor and the Publisher. Subscribers (listed in order of the receipt of their subscriptions) are:

JAMES LAUGHLIN (Norfolk)
MR. & MRS. ALFRED W. BROWN (Atlanta)
J.M. EDELSTEIN (Washington, DC)
DR. JOHN HARBERT (McLean)
JAMES MERRILL (Stonington)
ED ALBAUGH (Columbia)
MIKE & KATHY PAGE (Winston-Salem)
W. H. FERRY (Scarsdale)
DONALD B. ANDERSON (Roswell)
THEODORE & JOAN STEEN WILENTZ (Chevy Chase)
HERBERT LEIBOWITZ (New York City)
F. BORDEN HANES, JR. (Winston-Salem)
JOHN RUSSELL (Redding Ridge)
JEFFREY COOPER (Philadelphia)
THORNS & PERRY CRAVEN (Winston-Salem)
EDMOND FISHER (West Chester)
JOSEPH C. ANDERSON (Denver)
CHARLES HOWELL (Minneapolis)
MR. & MRS. GAIL H. ROUB (Fort Atkinson)
JAMES JAFFE (Haverford)
PETER QUARTERMAIN (Vancouver)
ALDEN ASHFORTH (Reseda)
MATTHEW & SHEILA JENNETT/PHAROS BOOKS (New Haven)
MICHAEL HOFFMAN (Shekomeko)
JOHN YAU (New York City)
WILLIAM HARTLEY (Winston-Salem)
SAMUEL LARCOMBE (Santa Fe)
PETER STRAUB (Green Farm)
ALFRED HIRSCH (New Haven)
ROGER CONOVER (Cambridge)
JEFFREY BEAM/STAN FINCH (Chapel Hill)
KATHLEEN KENNEDY TOWNSEND (Timonium)
STEPHEN JAMA II (Torrance)
DR. ROWLAND J. FULLILOVE (Chapel Hill)
ARTHUR M. JENS, JR. (Glen Ellyn)
ALEX GILDZEN (Kent)
R. PHILIP HANES, JR. (Winston-Salem)
KEITH SMITH (Rochester)
MRS. JACK H. WILCOX (Highlands)
BLACK MOUNTAIN COLLEGE COLLECTION/NC WESLEYAN
    COLLEGE (Rocky Mount)
DALE DAVIS (Fairport)
JEAN RIBOUD (New York City)
MARVIN & RUTH SACKNER (Miami Beach)
F. WHITNEY JONES (Winston-Salem)
MICHAEL GODFREY (Chapel Hill)
RAY KASS (Christiansburg)

TED POTTER (Winston-Salem)
JOHN OTIS KIRKPATRICK (Austin)
H. E. TURLINGTON, JR. (Pittsboro)
BARNEY B. HOLLAND, JR. (Fort Worth)
DANIEL HABERMAN (New York City)
GUY DAVENPORT (Lexington)
STEVEN CLAY (Minneapolis)
DAVID WILK (East Haven)
STEPHEN HARGRAVES (East Haven)
ARTHUR M. JENS, JR. (Chicago)
WILLIAM REES (New Haven)
AARON SISKIND (Providence)
LYLE BONGÉ (Biloxi)
GARY HOTHAM (New York City)
POETRY/RARE BOOKS COLLECTION, STATE UNIVERSITY OF NY
    (Buffalo)
LAUREL REUTER (Grand Forks)
IRWIN & BARBARA KREMEN (Durham)
ZORA HODGES MANLEY (Goldsboro)
BRADFORD MORROW (New York City)
SPECIAL COLLECTIONS, JACKSON LIBRARY, UNIVERSITY OF NC
    (Greensboro)
FORD BETTY FORD (Atlanta)
ANNE MIDGETTE (New York City)
SARAH ANDERSON (Kampsville)
DONALD B. ANDERSON, JR. (Casper)
KATHRYN SCHILT (Casper)
DAMERON MIDGETTE (Roswell)
RUTH PINNELL (Durham)
JOHN MENAPACE (Chapel Hill)
AM HERE BOOKS (Santa Barbara)
SUSAN COOPER (Denver)
SUZANNE BERNARDO (Winston-Salem)
TOM PATTERSON (Winston-Salem)
PACE TRUST (Louisville)
LUCINDA BUNNEN (Atlanta)
AMIE W. BLOCK (Washington, DC)
ROBYN JONES (Winston-Salem)
CHANDLER & MIEGAN GORDON/THE CAPTAIN'S BOOKSHELF
    (Asheville)
GAIL WHITNEY (Sacramento)
MR. & MRS. WALTER SCHEUER (New York City)
EUGENE RAMEY (San Francisco)